DOUBLES
FOR TAKEOUT,
PENALTIES AND
PROFIT
IN CONTRACT BRIDGE

by Robert B. Ewen

♠   ♡   ◇   ♣

PRENTICE-HALL, INC., ENGLEWOOD CLIFFS, N.J.

*Doubles for Takeout, Penalties and
Profit in Contract Bridge*
by Robert B. Ewen

Printed in the United States of America
10 9 8 7 6 5 4 3 2 1

Prentice-Hall International, Inc., *London*
Prentice-Hall of Australia, Pty., Ltd., *North Sydney*
Prentice-Hall of Canada, Ltd., *Toronto*
Prentice-Hall of India Private Ltd., *New Delhi*
Prentice-Hall of Japan, Inc., *Tokyo*

Library of Congress Cataloging in Publication Data
Ewen, Robert B.
   Doubles for takeout, penalties, and profit in
contract bridge.
    1. Contract bridge.   I. Title.
GV 1282.3.E89 1973   795.4'15   73-7756
ISBN 0-13-218834-1
ISBN 0-13-218826-0 (pbk.)

Introduction

Scarcely two years have passed since I had the pleasure of introducing Bob Ewen's first bridge book, *Opening Leads.* Although it was the fifth volume in the Prentice-Hall bridge series, it was the first under my aegis as Consulting Editor. Therefore, I am doubly delighted that it was instantly hailed as the classic in its field—the best, most complete, and most authoritative work on opening leads before or since.

Why, then, has it taken Dr. Ewen so long to produce another bridge book? There are many reasons. Foremost, perhaps, is the fact that he is what many might consider "fully employed" as associate professor of psychology at New York University. Then, of course, there's the urge to play and to talk about this game of bridge where his theories and his talents are widely recognized by his peers—the younger group of experts who have become so successful in the tournaments for which Bob himself has too little time. Again, there's the demand for his services as collaborator and editor of no fewer than three important bridge books to which he has made major contributions.

But most of all, I think the interval has been protracted by his need to meet his own standard of excellence, so clearly established in *Opening Leads.*

In this new book, Ewen has again selected a single vitally important segment of the game: the biggest potential profit-maker of all bids—the double. Again he has hit upon a subject which, despite the thousands of books written about bridge, has somehow been neglected. And again, as I think you will agree long before you have devoured this book, he has hit the bull's-eye.

You will find more things than you ever dreamed existed within the scope of the double and the collateral bids available for your choice, including cue bids and that wise but oft-neglected four letter word, "pass."

Are you a comparative novice? You will learn how to use

the double as a winning elementary tool. Are you an experienced player? This book is certain to double your winnings—or at least to halve your losses. Are you an expert? Set forth here are the newest methods from which you may choose and which your opponents may already be using against you.

Bridge, like war, is a constant armament's race: new means of defense against new methods of attack. I urge you to learn to wield the double-edged war ax so masterfully described here.

RICHARD L. FREY

Preface

This book is intended for any bridge player, from average-minus to expert, who wants better results at the bridge table and who is willing to invest a modicum of effort in order to achieve this end. The level of bridge competition has risen dramatically in the past fifteen years; for example, the highest ranking awarded by the American Contract Bridge League, Life Master, now includes some 15,000 members. (And the list is growing by leaps and bounds!) Even if you don't happen to aspire to this exalted status, you obviously must have something special going for you—some knowledge or ability that the typical player lacks—if you are not to fall by the wayside in your own bridge games.

Nowhere is the gap between the expert and the average player so great as in the area of doubles and competitive bidding. In my opinion, the reason for this is that most bridge writers regard this area as too difficult for anyone but an expert to absorb fully, so they settle for superficialities. This is unfortunate for several reasons. First, you *don't* have to be a genius to understand doubles and use them effectively *if* the subject is explained properly. (In fact, as one who has successfully taught college-level statistics for seven years to social science students with "mathematical blocks," I can testify that you don't need to be a mathematical wizard even to understand and use mathematics if it is presented correctly.) Second, the level of education in this country has risen along with the number of Life Masters, and the amount of available leisure time has also increased. Consequently, many people are turning to bridge who have sufficient ability and time to learn it with insight and play it with competence.

In this book, I have tried throughout to explain the *logic* of what you are asked to do along with the procedures themselves. For example, you are advised not only when to make a takeout double and when to prefer an overcall, but also *why* certain hands are better described by each bid. As a result, you will find it easier to make decisions about difficult in-between hands—those that contain some features which suggest a takeout double, but also have some aspects which would make an overcall desirable. Similarly, the factors that make a penalty double a good or bad risk are explained and illustrated so that you can apply what you learn to new situations that you encounter on your own. And since these principles have ramifications well beyond the area of competitive bidding, it's also possible that other aspects of your bridge game will benefit because you'll be learning how to think like the experts do.

You may not agree with everything you read in this book; I would rather include a few techniques that you'd prefer not to try than present a watered-down version that wouldn't give you much chance to hold your own at the bridge table even if you learned it all by heart. Adopt what seems right for you, and postpone anything else until and unless you are ready. (It took me several years to adopt negative doubles because they seemed so strange; but when I did, I was very happy with the results.) You needn't fear being left behind if you're starting from scratch, for all of the important basic ideas about doubles have been included. But you needn't be worried about an attack of boredom if you already know something about doubling, for many of the techniques that today's better players are winning with are simple enough so that they can be presented virtually at the outset.

I would like to take this opportunity to acknowledge the efforts of various people who contributed to the realization of this book and to the success of my first venture, *Opening Leads.* My path through the world of bridge has been greatly enriched by my contacts with such interesting and colorful characters as striped-tail apes, griffins, seals, snails, and whales. A special vote of thanks is due *The Bridge World* (39 West 94th Street, New York, N.Y. 10025, if you'd like to subscribe) for permission to use material from the world's leading source of innovative bridge ideas. This book has drawn upon modern techniques developed by some outstanding bridge theorists; I'm particularly indebted to Roger Stern, Edgar Kaplan, Lawrence Rosler, and Jeff Rubens. Dick Frey, the editor of the Prentice-Hall Contract Bridge Series and one of the original Life Masters (number 8, in fact), has been of considerable assistance in more ways than space permits mention, and Prentice-Hall has been a source of encouragement.

Lastly, but certainly not least, a warm vote of appreciation to my parents, for a great many reasons.

Bob Ewen

Contents

Introduction   iii

Preface   v

Prologue. Trouble Over Doubles   1

Part I. Takeout Doubles

   1.   Competing in Second Position   13
   2.   Competing in Fourth Position   73
   3.   Reopening and Negative Doubles   107

Part II. Penalty Doubles

   4.   Doubles for Penalties   135
   5.   Competitive Judgement   171
   6.   Lead-Directing Doubles   195

Part III. Informatory Doubles

   7.   Doubles of Unusual Opening Bids   219
   8.   Expert Tactics   239

Epilogue. Doubles for Profit   261

Index   275

Prologue

Trouble Over Doubles

♠ ♡ ◊ ♣

"I've got troubles," my bridge-addicted friend announced gloomily.

"What do you mean?" I asked. "I thought we had your opening leads all straightened out, and ..."

"Oh, my opening leads are fine," he interrupted. "It's doubles! They drive me crazy! Take a look at this hand:

> ♠ K 4 3
> ♡ A K Q 6 2
> ◊ 7
> ♣ Q 9 5 3

"My right-hand opponent opens the bidding with 1 ◊ , and that's that—I'm beaten before the deal has hardly begun. Whenever I make a takeout double with a hand like this, my left-hand opponent preempts by raising diamonds to some ridiculously high level and my partner chimes in with a bid of 3 ♠ or 4 ♠. I can't bid hearts now (that would promise at least a semi-solid six-card suit and would encourage partner to pass even with a singleton in support). So we play in spades, and partner turns up with:

> ♠ A 10 7 6
> ♡ 9 7 4
> ◊ 8 6 4
> ♣ K J 10

1

"Of course we go down; 4 ♡ would have been icy. And partner yells at me for suppressing my good suit. So the next time I face this situation, I overcall with 1 ♡. And what happens? My left-hand opponent bids 2 ◊, and my partner has no choice but to pass with:

> ♠ A 10 9 7 6
> ♡ 5
> ◊ 8 6 4 3
> ♣ K J 10

"After an *overcall*, he can't afford to bid spades with poor heart support and a weakish hand, for he may well be walking right into a disastrous misfit—and a substantial penalty. So this time we miss a probable spade game!"

"I remember some violent arguments about hands like this one in *The Bridge World* back around 1964," I said. "But . . ."

"And the same dilemma bugs me when I'm in the balancing position," my friend interrupted. "Suppose my *left*-hand opponent opens with 1 ◊, the next two players pass, and I'm in the fourth seat (vulnerable) holding:

> ♠ 9 3
> ♡ A K 7 4 2
> ◊ J
> ♣ A Q 10 9 2

"According to the bridge books, a simple overcall in this position shows a fairly weak hand, so I have to start with a double. But now the opening bidder gums up the works by jumping to 3 ◊ and my partner, confidently expecting support for all the unbid suits because of my double, bids 3 ♠! I try to extricate myself from this gory mess by bidding 4 ♣, suggesting to partner that he confine himself to a choice between clubs and hearts. But I wind up shelling out 500 points when the full deal turns out to be a disastrous misfit."

"But . . ." I said.

"And here's another doubling disaster," my irate friend intervened. "Even though declarer is an expert, wouldn't you expect to defeat a *six* spade contract holding Q J 10 8 of spades behind him and two side kings in addition? Well, I sure did, so I doubled! Here's the sad story:

NORTH
♠ K 9 7
♡ 9 8 2
◇ 7 5 4
♣ A Q 10 4

WEST (my friend)
♠ Q J 10 8
♡ K 10 3
◇ 9 8 2
♣ K 6 3

EAST
♠ —
♡ Q J 7 6 5 4
◇ 10 6 3
♣ 9 8 7 5

SOUTH
♠ A 6 5 4 3 2
♡ A
◇ A K Q J
♣ J 2

SOUTH	WEST	NORTH	EAST
1 ♠	Pass	2 ♠	Pass
3 ◇	Pass	4 ♣	Pass
6 ♠	Double	Pass	Pass
Pass			

"I led a diamond. South won, cashed the heart ace, finessed the queen of clubs, and ruffed a heart. He then played a trump to my ten and dummy's king, ruffed another heart, played a club to the ace, and ruffed a club. Finally, he cashed the king and queen of diamonds. When I followed to the third diamond, he lit up like a Christmas tree! The position at this point was:

NORTH
♠ 9 7
♡ —
◇ —
♣ 10

WEST
♠ Q J 8
♡ —
◇ —
♣ —

EAST
♠ —
♡ Q J
◇ —
♣ 9

SOUTH
♠ A 6
♡ —
◇ J
♣ —

"He led the jack of diamonds, and I was finished! If I ruff with the eight-spot, he overruffs with dummy's nine for the twelfth trick. So I trumped with the jack. He then pitched dummy's high but useless club, and I was endplayed. How's that for a lucky lie of the cards and a double-dummy line of play? If declarer draws even one round of trumps before cashing the ace of hearts, he's doomed!"

"But . . ." I said.

"And even when I do get a plus score with a double, it's a poor result," my friend went on inexorably. "My partner, vulnerable, opened the bidding with 1 ♠, my right-hand opponent overcalled 2 ◇, and I held:

♠ J 10 7 4
♡ J 9 8
◇ A K 3 2
♣ 10 9

"With four trumps to the ace-king opposite a partner who had opened the bidding, I was sure we had struck a bonanza, so I cracked it. But the full deal was:

                         NORTH
                         ♠ 9 6 3
                         ♡ K 7 6 5 4 2
                         ◊ 5
                         ♣ 7 5 2
WEST (my friend)   EAST
♠ J 10 7 4   ♠ A K Q 5 2
♡ J 9 8   ♡ A 3
◊ A K 3 2   ◊ 9 4
♣ 10 9   ♣ Q J 8 6
                         SOUTH (my friend)
                         ♠ 8
                         ♡ Q 10
                         ◊ Q J 10 8 7 6
                         ♣ A K 4 3

SOUTH	WEST	NORTH	EAST
—	—	—	1 ♠
2 ◊	Double	Pass	Pass
Pass			

"We wound up with six tricks and 100 points, but we should have won the rubber by bidding 4 ♠. And my partner had the nerve to yell at *me!*"

"But . . ." I said.

"Here's another example of the same thing," my friend broke in. "Anyone would expect to score a sizeable profit by defending against a *five* heart contract holding the ace of trumps, a side ace-king, and another king. But look what happened to me:

```
                    NORTH
                    ♠ Q J 7 3
                    ♡ 6 4
                    ◇ A Q J 5
                    ♣ A 3 2
WEST                                        EAST
♠ 10                                        ♠ 9 8 4
♡ K Q J 10 8 5 2                            ♡ 9 3
◇ —                                         ◇ 10 9 8 6 4 2
♣ Q 10 9 8 5                                ♣ K J
                    SOUTH (my friend)
                    ♠ A K 6 5 2
                    ♡ A 7
                    ◇ K 7 3
                    ♣ 7 6 4
```

SOUTH	WEST	NORTH	EAST
1 ♠	4 ♡	4 ♠	5 ♡
Double	Pass	Pass	Pass

"Who could expect that diamond void in the West hand?" my friend complained. "We scored another one-trick set, for another measly 100 points, instead of making another vulnerable game and winning another rubber. And my partner blamed me again!"

"But . . ." I said.

"And wouldn't you think that someone claiming to be a bridge player would know about lead-directing doubles? Look what my partner did to me on this hand!

NORTH
- ♠ J 8
- ♡ A K Q 6 3
- ◇ Q 10 8 2
- ♣ 6 4

WEST
- ♠ 7
- ♡ 9
- ◇ J 9 6 5 4 3
- ♣ K Q 8 5 2

EAST (my friend)
- ♠ A 4 2
- ♡ J 10 7 4 2
- ◇ —
- ♣ J 10 9 7 3

SOUTH
- ♠ K Q 10 9 6 5 3
- ♡ 8 5
- ◇ A K 7
- ♣ A

SOUTH	WEST	NORTH	EAST
1 ♠	Pass	2 ♡	Pass
3 ♠	Pass	4 ♠	Pass
4 NT	Pass	5 ◇	Double
6 ♠	Pass	Pass	Double
Pass	Pass	Pass	

"I thought partner should have jammed the auction with an unusual notrump," my friend argued, "but the way the bidding went made me very happy that he stayed silent. I doubled the 5 ◇ Blackwood response to tell partner what suit to lead, gambling that they couldn't play it there. And I doubled 6 ♣ because I saw a sure set. So what does my idiotic partner lead? A *club*! And they wrapped up the slam!"

"But . . ." I said.

"Nor was he satisfied with that disaster," my friend rushed on heedlessly. "Look what he did next!

NORTH
- ♠ A 3 2
- ♡ A 8 5
- ◇ A K 10 4
- ♣ K 6 5

WEST
- ♠ K Q J 10 8 7 5
- ♡ 4
- ◇ J 9 5
- ♣ 7 2

EAST
- ♠ 9
- ♡ K J 10 7 2
- ◇ Q 8 3
- ♣ Q J 10 8

SOUTH (my friend)
- ♠ 6 4
- ♡ Q 9 6 3
- ◇ 7 6 2
- ♣ A 9 4 3

SOUTH	WEST	NORTH	EAST
—	4 ♠	Double	Pass
5 ♡	Pass	Pass	Double
Pass	Pass	Pass	

"Of course I showed my major suit in response to my partner's double," my friend explained. "How could I expect such meager heart support? We were vulnerable again — and how! — so this delightful atrocity cost me a nice round 1100. And my partner, as usual, said (loudly!) that it was all my fault!"

"But . . ." I said.

"And the next deal was the very last straw!

```
                         NORTH
                         ♠  J 9 7 5
                         ♡  Q J 7 5
                         ◊  Q J 2
                         ♣  8 5
WEST (my friend)                          EAST
♠  10 8 3                                 ♠  A K Q 4 2
♡  A K 6 4 2                              ♡  10 8
◊  7                                      ◊  9 5 3
♣  A 10 4 2                               ♣  K Q 6
                         SOUTH
                         ♠  6
                         ♡  9 3
                         ◊  A K 10 8 6 4
                         ♣  J 9 7 3
```

SOUTH	WEST	NORTH	EAST
—	1 ♡	Pass	1 ♠
2 ◊	Pass	Pass	Double
Pass	Pass	Pass	

"I naturally sat for my partner's double with my three defensive tricks," my friend moaned. "But look at the junk he doubled on—three diamonds to the nine-spot! I went crazy

trying to beat the darned contract, but I can't find a way even
with all four hands exposed.* Besides, who wants to go through
all sorts of headsplitting analyses about a miserable two
diamond contract when we're cold for four spades? Phooey!"

"But . . ." I said.

"I'm fed up with doubles!" he proclaimed, continuing to
override any potential words of wisdom from me. "I'm going
home!"

And he did.

Some time later, Dick Frey phoned.

"Hi, Bob. How are things?"

"But . . ." I said, and trailed off wearily.

"How's that? We seem to have a bad connection. Hello?"

"I'm here," I said, finally escaping from my rut. "What's
up?"

"I've got an idea . . ."

The idea turned out to be this book on doubles, for the
problems that beset my friend are by no means trivial or
unusual ones. A great many bridge players find takeout doubles
frustrating, balancing doubles aggravating, penalty doubles
backfiring, low-level doubles humiliating, cooperative doubles
fired at uncooperative partners, and lead-directing doubles
eliciting every suit but the correct one. Perhaps you—like my
friend—have been tempted to abandon doubles in disgust.
Giving up such a valuable weapon, however, is losing bridge; in
fact, the ability to make killing doubles is one of the hallmarks
of the tough, feared player—one who allows opponents few if
any, liberties during the auction.

Therefore, the goal of this book is to explain how to use
doubles for takeout, penalties, cooperation, lead direction,
and—most importantly of all—for profit.

---

*Neither can I. If the defenders never play trumps, South simply wins
six trump tricks in his hand and two club ruffs in dummy. If West leads a
trump, South wins and leads a heart. West wins and plays a spade, East
wins and plays a trump, and South wins in his hand and plays another
heart. If West wins and goes passive, dummy's two heart tricks ensure the
contract. If West wins and leads a heart for East to ruff, South overruffs
and adds one high heart and a club ruff to his six trump tricks. And if West
ducks the heart, dummy wins and leads another heart; if East discards, so
does South.

Part **I.**

TAKEOUT DOUBLES

1

Competing in Second Position

♠ ♡ ◇ ♣

Suppose that your right-hand opponent opens the bidding with 1 ♡, and you hold either of these hands:

(a)   ♠   A K Q 10 2   (b)   ♠   A Q 8 7 3
        ♡   3   ♡   6 3
        ◇   Q 6 2   ◇   A K 4
        ♣   A 9 8 7   ♣   7 6 2

If you think this is a simple problem, you're in for a surprise! Let's listen in as Experts A and B, each representing a major school of thought, debate this innocuous-looking issue:

Expert A: "With these hands, you *must* make a takeout double! That will show a hand worth an opening bid and support for the unbid suits. If you overcall with 1 ♠ instead, partner is likely to pass with a singleton or void in spades and a respectable side suit of his own. You'll be in a terrible contract, and you'll deserve it for hogging the bidding."

Expert B: "With these hands, you *must* overcall with 1 ♠! That will enable you to find a 5-3 spade fit, and the spade suit is your most likely route to a part-score—or even a game. If you make a takeout double instead, partner probably won't bid spades with only a three-card suit; and if he responds 2 ♣ or 2 ◇, you won't have any idea what to do. If you pass, you may find him with 10 8 5 3 in his minor and K J 2 in spades; but if you return to spades, he may turn up with a singleton spade and a good long minor suit. In either case, you'll be in a terrible

13

contract, and you'll deserve it for confusing the bidding."

If you think ahead no further than your first competitive bid, this dilemma is indeed likely to appear insoluble. However, matters become much more straightforward—and only one of the above arguments remains tenable—if you correctly *plan two steps ahead* before entering the auction.

Double vs. Overcall: The Two Basic Patterns

THE TAKEOUT-DOUBLE PATTERN

At one end of the competitive bidding spectrum are hands that clearly require partner's cooperation in choosing the best suit for your side. For example, suppose your right-hand opponent opens the bidding with 1 ♡ and you hold either of these hands:

(a)	♠	K Q 3 2	(b)	♠	Q J 10 2
	♡	7		♡	—
	◊	A J 9 7		◊	A K J 6
	♣	J 10 8 7		♣	Q 9 7 4 3

In each case, you have excellent support for all of the unbid suits. Therefore, your best strategy is to leave the choice to your partner by making a *takeout double,* which asks him to select the unbid suit he most prefers.

THE OVERCALL PATTERN

At the other end of the spectrum are hands that require little if any cooperation from partner in picking the suit. For example, suppose your right-hand opponent opens with 1 ♡ and you hold:

(a) ♠ A K Q 9 7   (b) ♠ A K J 7 6 3
    ♥ 5 3 2   ♥ 6 4
    ♦ 10 7   ♦ A 3
    ♣ 10 8 6   ♣ 6 4 3

You have a strong preference for spades, so let partner know by making an *overcall* of 1 ♠. With an even more one-suit oriented hand, an even more dogmatic action is justified:

♠ K Q J 9 8 7 4 3
♥ 6 2
♦ 7
♣ 4 3

You should insist on playing in spades (if your side buys the contract) by making a preemptive overcall—3 ♠ if you are vulnerable and the opponents are not, and 4 ♠ otherwise. This action, just like a preemptive opening bid, tells partner not to bother bidding any suits of his own—even good ones!

In sum: With little preference among the unbid suits, obtain your partner's cooperation by making a takeout double. If you do have a strong preference, discourage him from bidding new suits by overcalling; in extreme cases, bar him from introducing new suits by preempting.

Your Strategy: Plan Two Steps Ahead

To return to our original problem, we saw that matters are not nearly so clear-cut when your right-hand opponent opens the bidding with 1 ♥ and you hold either of these hands:

(a) ♠ A K Q 10 2   (b) ♠ A Q 8 7 3
    ♥ 3   ♥ 6 3
    ♦ Q 6 2   ♦ A K 4
    ♣ A 9 8 7   ♣ 7 6 2

In each case, you would like to overcall 1 ♠ in order to emphasize your spade suit, but you would also like to enlist partner's cooperation by making a takeout double in case he has terrible spades and a good minor suit. Unfortunately, you can't bid "1 double ♠" on your first turn without running afoul of the laws of bridge (and your opponents). However, you can—and should—plan to make these two actions on your first *two* turns to bid—a legal (and effective) procedure. Here's how:

Step 1. First, overall 1 ♠. You must find a 5-3 spade fit if one exists, and partner probably won't bid a three-card spade suit in response to a takeout double. Therefore, bidding your good major suit takes top priority. It is true that partner will be discouraged from showing a minor suit of his own, but this disadvantage will (hopefully) only be temporary.

Step 2. If a good opportunity arises, make a takeout double at your *second* turn to bid (unless, of course, partner resolves your problems by raising spades). This will alert your partner to your secondary interest in the other unbid suits.

For example, the auction might proceed as follows:

YOU	LHO	PARTNER	RHO
—	—	—	1 ♡
1 ♠	2 ♡	Pass	Pass
Double			

or

YOU	LHO	PARTNER	RHO
—	—	—	1 ♡
1 ♠	Pass	Pass	2 ♡
Double			

This two-step strategy (overcalling 1 ♠ and then doubling if the auction permits) conveys the following message to your partner:

"Partner, I've got at least a pretty good five-card spade suit and a hand worth an opening bid. I've also got some support for the other unbid suits. Please raise spades with three-card or longer support instead of bidding some scraggly minor suit. But if your spade support is inadequate, bid your better minor. Of course, if you're loaded in hearts, you can pass for penalties; but you'd better have a lot of trump tricks because my double is intended for takeout."

Keep in mind that your two-step plan must take into consideration the strength of your hand. Suppose that the bidding proceeds:

YOU	LHO	PARTNER	RHO
—	—	—	1 ♡
1 ♠	3 ♡*	Pass	Pass
?	*Semipreemptive, not forcing.		

You should double holding

♠ A K Q 10 2
♡ 3
◇ Q 6 2
♣ A 9 8 7

Your strength will probably ensure safety for your side at the rarefied atmosphere of the three-level or four-level, and your initial spade bid will signal a safe landing place to partner if he is looking anxiously at a very weak hand. However, a discreet pass is in order holding

♠ A Q 8 7 3
♡ 6 3
◇ A K 4
♣ 7 6 2

Although you may not get the chance to take your second-round action in some cases, the two-step strategy will sharpen your competitive bidding by allowing you to put first things first while still retaining a good chance to describe the rest of your hand accurately. As we will see, there are times when you should:

> Overcall first and then double
> Double first and then overcall
> Pass first and then double
> Pass first and then overcall
> Just double
> Just overcall

However, there is no need to memorize a gigantic (and boring) list of bidding rules in order to keep these different situations straight. Instead, the examples that follow will familiarize you with the common types of hands and the reasoning that underlies the recommended action(s) in each case. (For example, one important principle is that since game in a major suit requires one trick less than game in a minor, high priority should be given to finding a 5-3 or 4-4 or better major-suit fit.) Once you get the general idea, you can have the fun (and profit) of extending the strategy to any new situations that you may encounter at the bridge table.

When to Double First

IDEAL TAKEOUT DOUBLES

The ideal pattern for a takeout double, as we have seen, consists of 4-4-4-1 or 5-4-4-0 distribution with the shortness in opener's suit. The double also promises a hand worth an opening bid, but the modern tendency is to shade this requirement somewhat because the ideal pattern offers such good support for any suit partner may bid. For example, make a takeout double of a 1 ◊ opening bid by your right-hand opponent if you hold:

♠ A 10 9 3
♡ K J 8 2
◊ 5
♣ Q 10 8 6

However, pass with

♠ Q J 3 2
♡ Q J 5 4
♢ 6
♣ K J 5 3

Don't enter the fight with no aces and only one king.* Also, be somewhat more conservative after your right-hand opponent opens with 1 ♠, for partner will have to bid a suit at the two-level in response to a takeout double.

The takeout double accurately describes your distribution, so your second step in the two-step strategy depends simply on your general strength. For example, if you make a takeout double of a 1 ♢ opening bid holding

♠ A K Q 3
♡ J 6 4 2
♢ 5
♣ Q 10 4 2

and partner responds 1 ♠ (the opponents remaining silent), you should pass. You have a minimal takeout double, so don't get excited just because partner hit your strongest suit. Remember, he *may* have as little as

♠ J 6 5 2
♡ 8 7 5
♢ 9 6 4 3
♣ 5 3

---

*Keep in mind that the standard 4-3-2-1 point count slightly undervalues aces and kings and slightly overvalues queens and jacks. Most of the time, this doesn't matter; but if you have a lot of queens and jacks, your hand is actually worth less than your total point count indicates. Similarly, if your point count consists mostly of aces and kings, your hand is worth more than your total point count indicates.

To raise a nonjump suit response, therefore, you need a powerful hand. For example, suppose your partner has responded 1 ♠ to your takeout double and you hold:

(a) ♠ A K 9 3   (b) ♠ A K 9 3   (c) ♠ A K Q 6
    ♡ K Q 10 7   ♡ K Q 10 4   ♡ A K 10 9
    ◇ 5   ◇ 5   ◇ 5
    ♣ K 10 7 4   ♣ A Q 4 2   ♣ K Q J 8

    Raise to 2 ♠   Raise to 3 ♠   Raise to 4 ♠
    (17 points)   (20 points)   (24 points)

Note that even with a magnificent collection like hand (c), 4 ♠ may go down if partner has a Yarborough!

IMPERFECT TAKEOUT DOUBLES

Some hands that don't meet the ideal takeout double pattern are so close to it that the difference is negligible. For example:

RHO opens 1 ◇
♠ K Q 9 2
♡ A J 8 7
◇ 6 3
♣ K 10 9

An immediate takeout double is best because you have four-card support for any unbid *major* suit and at least three-card support for the unbid minor, plus a hand that is clearly worth an opening bid. (It's inadvisable to make an "imperfect" takeout double with less than 13 points.) You should also double a 1 ◇ opening bid if you hold:

♠ K Q 9
♡ A J 8 7
◇ 6 3
♣ K 10 9 2

Your spade support, while only three cards in length, is very strong. The following situations, however, are not as clear:

(a) RHO opens 1 ♡   (b) RHO opens 1 ♣   (c) RHO opens 1 ♠
  ♠ 4 3 2   ♠ K 10 4 2   ♠ 8 3 2
  ♡ 4 2   ♡ A J 6 2   ♡ Q 4 3
  ◇ A K J 9   ◇ 4 2   ◇ A J 6 5
  ♣ K Q 10 8   ♣ A Q 3   ♣ A K 2

Each of these hands has a serious drawback that makes a takeout double risky. Hand (a) has very weak support for the unbid major; a diamond response on hand (b) will be distinctly embarrassing; and hand (c) has terrible distribution as well as only three-card support for the unbid major. If, however, you pass up this cheap opportunity to let partner know that you have a hand worth an opening bid, you may never get another safe chance to announce your strength, and your side may miss a good partial (or perhaps even a game) because partner isn't good enough to contest the auction all by himself.

In truth, there is no right answer in these situations. Aggressive experts would double; more conservative players would pass. It is up to you and your partner to select the style best suited to your temperament and ability. One word of warning: It's almost always best to avoid a takeout double with only two cards or less in an unbid major suit. Experience has made clear, however, that passing with very strong hands (a good 16 points or more) is all too likely to cause your side to miss a good contract. Therefore, you should make a takeout double of a 1 ♣ opening bid if you hold

  ♠ A Q J 2
  ♡ A Q 10
  ◇ A 3 2
  ♣ 5 4 2

Your extra strength will compensate for your imperfect distribution. But don't double a 1 ♣ opening bid holding

♠ K Q 2
♡ Q 6 3
◇ A 10 6 5
♣ A Q 10

A more descriptive alternative exists: an overcall of 1 NT, showing 16 — 18 high-card points, stoppers in the enemy suit, and a balanced hand. If you hold

♠ K 7 3
♡ K Q 9
◇ A Q J
♣ A J 10 8

you can show your additional strength by doubling the 1 ♣ opening bid and then bidding notrump. This two-step strategy shows a hand similar to a 1 NT overcall, but worth 19—21 points.

As was the case with "ideal" takeout doubles, your second step after "imperfect" doubles depends on your general strength. Thus, a single raise of a nonjump suit bid by partner shows about 17 points, a double raise shows about 20 points, and a triple raise to 4 ♡ or 4 ♠ requires about 23 points. Be cautious if partner bids a suit for which you have only three-card support, however, since he is bidding under compulsion and his suit may therefore be very weak. (In fact, there are some emergencies in which he is forced to bid a three-card suit!) Also, keep a sharp eye out for imaginative rebids such as the following:

YOU	LHO	PARTNER	RHO
—	—	—	1 ♡
Double	2 ♡	3 ♣	Pass
?			

You hold:

♠ A K Q J
♡ 7 6 3
◊ K Q
♣ K 8 5 2

A quick decision to play in clubs may seem justified in view of your fine support, but such haste will lead to a great deal of waste. The opponents have bid and raised hearts and you have three of them, so partner shouldn't have more than a doubleton; partner was under no compulsion to act because of the 2 ♡ bid and yet introduced clubs at the three-level, so he should have a strong suit; and your spade suit is absolutely solid. These clues indicate that you should proceed directly to your only makable game: Bid 4 ♠! Partner's hand:

♠ 4 3 2
♡ 4 2
◊ 7 6
♣ A Q 9 7 4 3

DOUBLING AND THEN OVERCALLING

Some hands are primarily oriented toward a takeout double, but also contain a good long suit. For example:

(a) RHO opens 1 ♠   (b) RHO opens 1 ♣
    ♠ —   ♠ A 7 6 4
    ♡ A Q 7 6   ♡ A J 5
    ◊ K 9 3   ◊ A J 10 9 6
    ♣ K Q 10 8 7 5   ♣ 3

Your long minor suit in each case is strong enough for an overcall, but investigating a possible 4-4 major-suit fit is more likely to pay rich dividends. You have adequate support for all unbid suits, so you should start with a takeout double. If partner bids your four-card major suit, you'll be in fine shape; if he doesn't, you may well be able to mention your long minor later on. For example, the auction on hand (a) may proceed:

YOU	LHO	PARTNER	RHO
—	—	—	1 ♠
Double	2 ♠	Pass	Pass
?			

The opponents have found a fit, which makes it more likely that your side has one also; they have stopped well short of game; and you have a powerful hand. Therefore, it is too soon to give up the ship (and the auction), and you should bid 3 ♣.

If instead the auction had proceeded

YOU	LHO	PARTNER	RHO
—	—	—	1 ♠
Double	2 ◇	Pass	2 ♡
?			

you should pass. The opponents should have most of the outstanding strength; and they have not yet found any fit, so the deal may well be a serious misfit for all concerned — and a disaster for whichever side declares the contract.

While partner may bid hearts in response to your double with hand (b), this need not be a cause for concern because your three-card support is strong. If the combined holding is

YOU	PARTNER
♠ A 7 6 4	♠ 8 3 2
♡ A J 5	♡ K Q 4 2
◇ A J 10 9 6	◇ K Q 3
♣ 3	♣ 6 4 2

a 4 ♡ contract will be ideal. And if instead partner remains silent, you can still introduce your diamond suit if the auction proceeds:

YOU	LHO	PARTNER	RHO
–	–	–	1 ♣
Double	2 ♣	Pass	Pass
2 ◇			

However, the following hand requires a different strategy:

♠ A 7 6 4
♡ A J 5
◇ 3
♣ A J 10 9 6

If your right-hand opponent opens with 1 ◇, you double, your left-hand opponent bids 2 ◇, and this is passed back to you, you should double *again* in order to let partner compete at the two-level if his hand is weak. A club bid would squander a whole level of bidding, and your suit is not noteworthy enough for such extravagance.

Some two-suited hands also qualify for the double-and-then-overcall treatment. For example:

♠ K J 9 7
♡ 6 4
◇ A Q J 9 8 2
♣ 8

After a 1 ♡ opening bid by your right-hand opponent, you would like to try for a spade contract by making a takeout double, but you would also like to advertise your powerful diamond suit by overcalling. Since you are fortunate enough to hold your length in the two *higher*-ranking unbid suits, you can do both. First, make a takeout double; if partner responds in spades or (improbably) in diamonds, all will be well. If he misguidedly mentions clubs, however, simply direct his attention to the other two unbid suits by converting to diamonds:

YOU	LHO	PARTNER	RHO
—	—	—	1 ♡
Double	Pass	2 ♣ (or 3 ♣)	Pass
2 ◊ (or 3 ◊)			

Should partner remain silent and the opponents peter out at a low level after finding a fit, you can still show your diamonds:

YOU	LHO	PARTNER	RHO
—	—	—	1 ♡
Double	2 ♡	Pass	Pass
3 ◊			

However, be careful not to confuse the preceeding hand with one like:

    ♠ K J 9 7
    ♡ 6 4
    ◊ 8
    ♣ A Q J 9 8 2

Here you cannot afford an initial takeout double of a 1 ♡ opening bid. If partner makes a jump response of 3 ◊ (which is by no means unlikely), you will have to bid 4 ♣ and thus reach the four-level on a possible misfit. The difficulty in this case is that you must *increase the level of bidding* in order to convert to your long suit, and the reason for this unhappy state of affairs is that you do *not* hold your length in the two *higher*-ranking unbid suits. A special convention called the Astro Cue-Bid (described later in this chapter) has been developed for just such hands; if you prefer natural methods, overcall 2 ♣ and hope for the best.

When to Pass First

It is usually a good idea to stay out of the auction — at least for a while — when you have length and strength in the suit bid by your right-hand opponent. After all, most of the cards in this suit have been accounted for by his bid and your length, so your left-hand opponent is likely to be short in it, long in your suit (since his cards have to be somewhere), and thirsting to make a devastating penalty double. The deal is probably a misfit for both sides, so your best strategy should be to lie low and let the opponents go down in some ill-fated contract of their own. At a subsequent stage of the auction, however, it may be desirable to insert a competitive bid.

PASSING AND THEN DOUBLING

Suppose your right-hand opponent opens the bidding with 1 ◇ and you hold

> ♠ A 10 8 7
> ♡ J 7 5 2
> ◇ A K 10 6
> ♣ A

Your distribution is wrong for a takeout double and is too unbalanced for a notrump overcall, so you should pass and hope for a better chance to enter the auction later on. This will be possible if the auction proceeds

YOU	LHO	PARTNER	RHO
—	—	—	1 ◊
Pass	1 NT	Pass	2 ♣
Double			

or even

YOU	LHO	PARTNER	RHO
—	—	—	1 ◊
Pass	2 ♣	Pass	2 ◊
Double			

Your two-step strategy of passing and then doubling after a *new* suit has been introduced shows a good takeout double of the new suit (in this case, clubs). Therefore, it implies strength in the suit first bid by the enemy (diamonds). However, be forewarned that you need a strong hand for this double (at least 16 points), for you are asking partner to bid at the two-level on a deal that may well be a misfit.

Here's another example:

♠   —
♡   A K 4 3
◊   A K 6
♣   Q J 10 7 5 2

If you are happily contemplating this impressive collection only to hear your right-hand opponent open the bidding with 1 ♣, don't go into traumatic shock! First of all, psychiatric treatment is rather expensive these days; but even worse, such an extreme reaction will tip your hand to the opponents. A takeout double with a void in the unbid spade suit would be egregious and a 2 ♣ overcall would be a cue-bid, so pass calmly and smoothly. If your left-hand opponent now responds 1 ♠, your partner passes, and your right-hand opponent raises to 2 ♠, however, you should enter the auction with a takeout double. You are strong enough to compel your partner to bid at the three-level, and you have a fine takeout double of spades.

Doubles such as these are best reserved for strong hands — ones on which it would be downright painful to pass throughout the auction. Also, don't confuse the preceding situations with auctions like the following ones:

(a)	YOU	LHO	PARTNER	RHO
	—	—	—	1 ♡
	Pass	2 ♡	Pass	Pass
	Double			

(b)	YOU	LHO	PARTNER	RHO
	—	—	—	1 ♠
	Pass	1 NT	Pass	2 ♠
	Double			

In each case, only one suit has been bid, so you cannot possibly have discovered a good takeout double that didn't exist on the first round. The double in auction (a) is a straightforward takeout double that simply attempts to avoid selling out too cheaply. The double in auction (b) is strictly for penalties and indicates that you trap-passed on the first round with a good hand, and long and strong spades.

PASSING AND THEN OVERCALLING

Suppose your right-hand opponent opens with 1 ♣ and you hold:

♠ K J 10 8 2
♡ 7
♢ 6 3
♣ A Q 9 8 3

You should pass. Your spade suit is strong enough for an overcall, but your length in opener's club suit warns that the hand may be a dangerous misfit. But suppose the auction proceeds:

YOU	LHO	PARTNER	RHO
—	—	—	1 ♣
Pass	1 ◇	Pass	1 ♡
?			

If you are not vulnerable, a 1 ♠ overcall at this point is reasonable because it shows both of your long suits. Why? With an ordinary overcall, you would have bid 1 ♠ directly over 1 ♣. Therefore, your two-step strategy of passing and then overcalling shows length in the suit you bid *and* the suit first bid by the enemy, and gives partner two choices insofar as contesting the auction is concerned.

BALANCING IN SECOND POSITION

Most of the time, your initial pass will be caused by weakness, rather than by length in the enemy suit. Even in such cases, however, it may pay to get into the auction later on. For example:

YOU	LHO	PARTNER	RHO
—	—	—	1 ♡
Pass	2 ♡	Pass	Pass
?			

You hold:

♠ K 8 6 5
♡ 7
◇ Q 9 6 2
♣ K 10 8 3

When the opponents find a fit, yet throw in the towel at a low level of bidding, your side is very likely to have a fit also, plus a fair share of strength. Therefore, while you were clearly too weak for a first-round takeout double, you should double now. This balancing double is for takeout and shows good support for all unbid suits, although you may (as usual) be somewhat below par in an unbid *minor*. It also promises about 10 points — a little more if you are doubling the raise to 2 ♠ and partner will have to respond at the three-level, and a little less if the opponents have stopped in 2 ♣ and partner is certain to be able to respond at the two-level.

If instead you hold an overcall-oriented hand that was too weak for action on the first round, like

♠ Q 8 7 6 2
♡ 8 7 3
◇ A J
♣ 10 8 2

balance in your long suit by bidding 2 ♠. You have a strong preference among the unbid suits, so there is no need to solicit partner's cooperation.

When the opponents have *not* found a good suit fit, it will usually be better to stay on the sidelines. For example:

YOU	LHO	PARTNER	RHO
—	—	—	1 ♠
Pass	1 NT	Pass	Pass
?			

Here, the deal may well be a misfit for both sides, so balancing is fraught with danger. In fact, a double on this auction shows a strong hand—one well worth an opening bid—and indicates you were trap-passing on the first round of bidding. Your double is for penalties, although partner may pull it with a weak hand and a long suit.

At rubber bridge, pass rather than balance in a close situation; it doesn't make sense to go down 1400 trying for a part-score. A well-timed balance, however, can be highly infuriating to opponents with meager values who were hoping to steal a partial.

When to Overcall First

IDEAL OVERCALLS

Ideal overcalls come in four different varieties:

1. *Preemptive overcalls.* As we have seen, you should insist on playing in your suit when you have a strongly one-suited hand like

♠   K Q J 9 8 7 4 3
♥   6 2
♦   7
♣   4 3

If your right-hand opponent opens the bidding with one of a suit, you should make a preemptive overcall—3 ♠ if you are vulnerable and the opponents are not, and 4 ♠ otherwise.* This is an ideal overcall: It tells partner that you don't need his cooperation in choosing the best suit for your side, it will disrupt the opponents' bidding, and it is reasonably safe. Holding

♠   K Q J 9 8 7 4
♥   6 2
♦   7
♣   10 4 3

---

*The standard practice is to be within two tricks of your preempt if you are vulnerable (for example, have eight tricks for a 4 ♠ preempt) and three tricks if you are not vulnerable (have seven tricks for a 4 ♠ preempt). Modern experts tend to be somewhat more aggressive than this, however, especially in match-point pairs tournaments where the cost of one disastrous set is not so great as it is in rubber bridge.

you should preempt by one trick less — for example, overcall
3 ♠ with neither side vulnerable — because you have one less
playing trick.

Once you have made a preemptive overcall, *don't* take any
further action unless partner makes a forcing bid. The following
ranks among the most heinous crimes in bridge:

SOUTH	WEST	NORTH	EAST
—	—	—	1 ♡
3 ♠	4 ♡	4 ♠	5 ♡
5 ♠??	Double	*#$!*!!	

North was able to defeat 5 ♡ in his own hand, having
cleverly boosted the opponents just high enough. But South
spoiled his partner's plan by telling the same story twice,
thereby turning a plus score into a minus. The moral: After a
preempt, leave all future decisions to your partner; he knows
your hand a great deal better then you know his.

2. *Weak jump overcalls.* Suppose your right-hand opponent
opens with one of a suit and you hold, not vulnerable:

♠ K Q J 9 8 7
♡ 6 2
◇ 7 3
♣ 10 4 3

Here again, your hand is ideal for a preemptive overcall—a
long and strong suit and poor defensive strength—but you are
not strong enough to bid at the three-level with only five
playing tricks. The solution to this vexing situation is to use
preemptive single jump overcalls. Thus, a 2 ♠ overcall with the
above hand shows a preemptive overcall that is too weak by one
trick to be made at the three-level. This allows you to gain the
advantages mentioned previously: informing your partner that

spades is likely to be the best spot for your side even if he has poor support, interfering with the enemy bidding, and relative safety.*

As with any preemptive overcall, don't bid again after a weak jump overcall unless partner directly solicits your co-operation by making a forcing bid. Also, *don't* make a weak jump overcall with a hand like

♠   9 8 6 5 3 2
♡   A 6
◊   7 2
♣   A 4 2

If your right-hand opponent opens with one of a suit, you should pass. You have a poor suit and good defensive strength — exactly the opposite of a preemptive overcall!

3. *Regular overcalls.* After a 1 ♡ opening bid on your right, you should overcall 1 ♠ with either of these hands:

(a)   ♠ A K Q 9 7   (b)   ♠ A K J 7 6 3
       ♡ 5 3 2   ♡ 6 4
       ◊ 10 7   ◊ A 3
       ♣ 10 8 6   ♣ 6 4 3

*About ten years ago, some strong but poorly reasoned attacks were made on weak jump overcalls. These criticisms overlooked several crucial points: (1) Preemptive three-level and four-level overcalls are in universal use, and weak jump overcalls are similar except that they are made one level lower and show one trick less; (2) while strong jump overcalls are useful when you have a 19-point hand with a six-card suit or a strong two-suiter, such hands arise rarely, and hands suitable for weak jump overcalls are much more common; (3) when you use weak jump overcalls, your regular overcalls now promise a fairly decent hand (since you *didn't* make a W.J.O.), which is very helpful to partner in selecting his response and acting over further competition by the opponents. For these reasons, the majority of today's bridge experts use weak jump overcalls.

You are most interested in your long and strong suit, and the overcall properly conveys this message.

Be careful not to overcall at the *two*-level unless you have considerable playing strength. For example, pass a 1 ♡ opening bid on your right if you hold

♠ K 2
♡ 5 4 3
◇ Q 6 3
♣ A Q 8 3 2

Opponents are much more prone to double for penalties at the two-level than the one-level, and your club suit is weak. (Switch the clubs and spades, however, and a 1 ♠ overcall is correct.) For a 2 ♣ overcall, you should have at least

♠ K 2
♡ 5 4
◇ Q 10 3
♣ A Q 10 9 7 6

or

♠ 9 2
♡ A J 2
◇ 10 6 3
♣ A K J 9 7

Your rebids after a regular overcall depend in large part on your partner's response (if any). Therefore, give close attention to the meanings of responses to an overcall, which will be discussed later in this chapter.

4. *Super-strong overcalls.* Suppose that your right-hand opponent deals and opens the bidding with 1 ♡, and you are the lucky holder of either of the following hands:

(a) ♠ K Q J 8 7 6 3   (b) ♠ A K 9 7 6
     ♡ A 6   ♡ K 10 8
     ◊ 7   ◊ A 10 9 5
     ♣ K J 2   ♣ A

Both hands are so strong that special measures are
required, for partner might pass a mere 1 ♠ overcall when your
side is cold for the game. Since a jump overcall would be
preemptive, an alternative strategy must be found for this
(infrequent) situation, and the solution is simply to double first
and then jump in your long suit:

YOU	LHO	PARTNER	RHO
—	—	—	1 ♡
Double	Pass	2 ♣	Pass
3 ♠			

The two-step strategy of doubling and then jumping in a
new suit shows a super-strong overcall of about 19 points or
more, and strongly urges (but does not force) partner to bid. It
does *not* show a takeout double pattern; the second bid (jump
in your suit) cancels that message.

Of course, you should modify your plan to jump at your
next turn when the auction so dictates:

YOU	LHO	PARTNER	RHO
—	—	—	1 ♡
Double	3 ♡	Pass	Pass
?			

In this auction, a bid of 3 ♠ is quite sufficient to show
your strength, since you are acting freely at the three-level
opposite a passed partner.

IMPERFECT OVERCALLS

Most bridge books frown upon overcalling in four-card suits, but experts know there are times when it is desirable to do so. For example, suppose your right-hand opponent opens with 1 ♣ and you hold:

    ♠ A Q 10 2
    ♡ 7 3
    ◊ K Q 9
    ♣ 6 4 3 2

A takeout double is unthinkable with only two-card support for an unbid major. You could pass, but a 1 ♠ overcall is likely to work out well. You have a *strong* four-card *major* suit, and you can bid at the *one*-level; also, you can block out two possible responses by your left-hand opponent (1 ◊ and 1 ♡), which may well cause him considerable difficulty. (A 1 ♠ overcall of a 1 ♡ opening bid would have less to gain, since it probably wouldn't keep your left-hand opponent from doing whatever he would have done without your overcall.) To provide the necessary margin of safety, however, don't overcall in a four-card suit unless you can do so at the one-level.

OVERCALLING AND THEN DOUBLING

We have seen that hands like the ones presented at the beginning of this chapter are best handled by first overcalling and then, if the auction permits, making a subsequent takeout double. The immediate overcall enables you to find a 5-3 major-suit fit if one exists, and the second-round takeout double alerts partner to your secondary interest in the other unbid suits. Here are some more examples:

(a) RHO opens 1 ♠   (b) RHO opens 1 ♠   (c) RHO opens 1 ◊

  ♠ 3   ♠ 3   ♠ 3

  ♡ A K J 9 5   ♡ A K 7 6 4 2   ♡ A 4 2

  ◊ 7 4 2   ◊ K J 3   ◊ A J 3

  ♣ A Q 5 4   ♣ K 10 2   ♣ A J 10 7 4 2

With hands (a) and (b), your first step is to overcall 2 ♡. Then, if a good opportunity arises later on (and partner hasn't supported hearts), make a takeout double. With hand (c), your long suit is (unfortunately) a minor; but it is a good *six*-carder, and you have only *three*-card support for the unbid major. Therefore, top priority should be given to the 2 ♣ overcall. You will watch for an opportunity to make a subsequent takeout double, which will let partner know that you are moderately interested in the red suits. If instead you hold

                  ♠ 3

                  ♡ 6 4 2

                  ◊ A J 3

                  ♣ A J 10 7 4 2

you should also begin with a 2 ♣ overcall – and end with it. Your distribution is correct for a subsequent takeout double, but you are not strong enough to act twice opposite a silent partner.

Priorities can easily get confused when you hold 5-4 distribution in the major suits:

(a) RHO opens 1 ♣   (b) RHO opens 1 ♡   (c) RHO opens 1 ◊

  ♠ A K Q 3 2   ♠ 9 8 7 6 3   ♠ A K Q 3 2

  ♡ J 4 3 2   ♡ A K J 4   ♡ J 4 3 2

  ◊ 7   ◊ 7   ◊ 7 5

  ♣ A 4 3   ♣ A Q 3   ♣ A 4

You have a very close decision with hand (a). A 1 ♠ overcall gives you the best chance to find a 5-3 spade fit, and you may still be able to make a takeout double later on. An immediate takeout double, however, is more likely to locate a 4-4 heart fit. As the saying goes, "You pays your money and you takes your choice." With hand (b), however, the spade suit is much too weak for an overcall, so an initial takeout double is your best choice. And with hand (c), a club response to a takeout double will be awkward, so here the balance shifts in favor of a direct 1 ♠ overcall.

Cue-Bids

Once upon a time, a 2 ♡ overcall of a 1 ♡ opening bid showed a hand worth an opening strong two-bid. Eventually, it occurred to bridge theorists that this situation occurred about once every four years, and so a perfectly useful bid was going to waste. Consequently, almost all of today's experts attach a special meaning to the direct cue-bid. Some of the most popular are:

1. *Michaels Cue-Bid.* This cue-bid, devised by the late Mike Michaels, shows a two-suited hand. A cue-bid of 2 ♣ or 2 ◊ promises at least 5-5 in the major suits. A cue-bid of 2 ♡ or 2 ♠ shows at least five cards in the unbid major and a five-card or longer minor suit. Thus, a Michaels Cue-Bid always shows as many long major suits as possible. For example:

(a) RHO opens 1 ◊	(b) RHO opens 1 ♠	(c) RHO opens 1 ◊
♠ A Q 8 6 2	♠ A 10 8 6 2	♠ 7
♡ K J 9 6 5	♡ 6	♡ A Q 10 6 4
◊ 6 3	◊ Q J 9 6 5 2	◊ 7 3
♣ 7	♣ 7	♣ K Q 7 6 2

A Michaels Cue-Bid of 2 ♣ is appropriate with hand (a), showing a major two-suiter. A 2 ♡ cue-bid is proper with hand (b). With hand (c), however, your shortness in an unbid major prohibits a cue-bid, so you should simply overcall 1 ♡.

2. *Astro Cue-Bid.* The Astro Cue-Bid, developed by Paul Allinger, Roger Stern, and Lawrence Rosler, also shows a two-suited hand. However, it always promises one major suit

and one minor suit. Also, the major is exactly four cards long, while the minor is either six cards in length or a very strong five-carder. More specifically:

Cue-Bid	Suits Promised
2 ♣	4 hearts and 5 or 6 diamonds
2 ♦	4 hearts and 5 or 6 clubs
2 ♡	4 spades and 5 or 6 clubs
2 ♠	4 hearts and 5 or 6 clubs

One way to remember this apparently complicated table is that an Astro Cue-Bid promises hearts and clubs unless the opponents have bid one of them, in which case it shows instead the other major or minor. The purpose of the Astro Cue-Bid is to enable you to describe a particular kind of hand that is awkward to cope with by any other method. For example, we saw earlier that a takeout double of 1 ♡ is inadvisable holding

    ♠ K J 9 7
    ♡ 6 4
    ♦ 8
    ♣ A Q J 9 8 2

Much as you would like to find a 4-4 spade fit, you cannot risk a 3 ♦ response to your takeout double, which would force you to soar to 4 ♣ on a possible misfit. The Astro Cue-Bid of 2 ♡ resolves this problem by immediately announcing four spades and six clubs. If partner has a four-card or longer spade suit, he bids it; if not, he can bid clubs at the three-level.

Note that with four spades and six *diamonds,* you don't need special methods because you can start with a takeout double and convert a club response to diamonds; and with 5-5 distribution, you can make an immediate spade overcall. Your problems are most serious when you have 4-6 or 4-5 distribution which is *not* in the two higher-ranking unbid suits, and it is precisely this situation which the Astro Cue-Bid is designed to handle.

3. *Roth Cue-Bid.* This cue-bid, invented by Alvin Roth, shows either ideal takeout double distribution and 19 points or more, or imperfect takeout double distribution and 20 points or more. For example, either of the following two hands would be a minimum 2 ◊ cue-bid of a 1 ◊ opening bid by your right-hand opponent:

(a) ♠   A K 8 7   (b) ♠   A K 8 5
      ♡   K Q J 7   ♡   K Q J 6
      ◊   6   ◊   7 4
      ♣   K J 10 8   ♣   A Q 4

The Roth Cue-Bid has two advantages. It is uncomplicated; and it enables you to make a light takeout double more safely, since the failure to cue-bid limits your hand to 18 or 19 points. A disadvantage is that strong hands like these are rather infrequent.

4. *Strong Two-Suited Cue-Bid.* Some experts use the cue-bid to show a strong two-suited hand. For example, after a 1 ◊ opening bid by your right-hand opponent, a 2 ◊ cue-bid shows a hand like

      ♠   K Q 8 6 3
      ♡   A
      ◊   7
      ♣   A K J 7 5 4

If partner makes the probable 2 ♡ response, you bid 3 ♣ to insist on a choice between the two remaining suits. (The alternative way to bid this hand, for those who prefer to use one of the other cue-bids, is to double first and then cue-bid diamonds over a heart response to demand an alternative selection.)

5. *Natural Cue-Bid.* Some players treat the cue-bid as a natural overcall, even though it is a bid in the enemy suit. This may be useful against opponents who frequently open three-card minors, and perhaps against those who open four-card majors. Needless to say, a powerful suit is essential!

Sizing Up the Opponents, Your Partner, the Vulnerability, and the Form of Scoring

Before leaving the chair of the doubler or overcaller to see how things look from the other side of the table, it should be noted that bridge is a game of personalities as well as of skill. Thus, when you are faced with a close decision, a knowledge of the opponents' bridge habits—and your partner's—will be extremely helpful in deciding whether or not to risk entering the auction.

If your opponents are hair-trigger penalty doublers and superb defenders, let discretion be the better part of valor and pass in borderline situations. If, however, your opponents are genial folks who rarely mention the word "double" and who generously drop a few tricks on defense every so often, you can afford to resolve a close issue in favor of the aggressive action.

Similarly, if your partner is a poor dummy player or a notorious overbidder, you're only asking for trouble if you enter the auction without solid values. If partner is a strong player, however, you can afford to compete more often; and you can make takeout doubles somewhat more readily than you would ordinarily, for your expert partner will know how to play a 4-3 major-suit fit if he winds up in one. Finally, whether partner is novice or expert, be more conservative if he has passed originally; if game is out of reach for your side, you have less to gain by entering the auction.

Close decisions about whether or not to compete are also affected by impersonal considerations such as vulnerability. If you are vulnerable, don't overcall or make a takeout double unless you have your full quota of strength and thus see at least some chance for game. If you are not vulnerable, however, you can afford to shade your overcalls and takeout doubles somewhat, especially if the opponents are vulnerable.

The form of scoring is also an important factor. Be more conservative at rubber bridge; don't risk a huge penalty just to try for a part-score. In match-point pairs tournaments, however, you should be more aggressive. Incurring one large penalty is not ruinous, for it can be recouped on the very next hand by making one 30-point overtrick more than everybody else; and you must try to induce the opponents to make mistakes against you if you are to have any chance to win.

Responding to a Takeout Double

Now let's move across the table and assume that your partner has inserted a competitive bid in second position. If he has made a takeout double, you must comply with his request to bid even if your hand is pitifully weak. For example, if the auction proceeds

YOU	LHO	PARTNER	RHO
—	1 ♠	Double	Pass
?			

and you are unlucky enough to hold

♠ 4 3 2
♡ 4 3 2
◇ 4 3 2
♣ 5 4 3 2

bid 2 ♣. A pass would be highly infuriating to your partner and most gratifying to the opponents, for they would undoubtedly wrap up the doubled 1 ♠ contract (probably with lucrative overtricks). Partner must allow for the possibility that your hand is very weak, because your bid was made under compulsion.

Since you must respond even with zero points, you should take special action when you do have useful values in order to alert partner to the possibility of game:

Response to Takeout Double	*Meaning*
Nonjump bid of new suit	0-8 points; usually a four-card or longer suit, but may be only a three-carder.
Jump in new suit	9-11 points, not forcing; usually a good four-card or longer suit.
Cue-bid of enemy suit	12 or more points; forcing.
1 NT	7-10 high-card points; good stoppers in enemy suit; balanced hand.
2 NT	11-13 high-card points; good stoppers in enemy suit; balanced hand.
Pass	*Solid* trump suit (K Q J 10 2 or better); orders partner to lead a trump.

The following are some illustrative examples. In each case, the auction has proceeded as follows:

YOU	LHO	PARTNER	RHO
—	1 ♡	Double	Pass
?			

(a)   ♠ J 9 7 6
       ♡ 6 3 2
       ◊ A 10 8 7 2
       ♣ 5

Bid 1 ♠. Help locate a 4-4 major-suit fit by giving the spades top priority, even though the diamonds are better.

(b)   ♠ 5
      ♡ 6 3 2
      ◊ A 10 8 7 2
      ♣ J 9 7 6

Bid 2 ◊. When choosing among two minor or two major suits, select the longer one.

(c)   ♠ J 9 7
      ♡ Q 10 9 3 2
      ◊ 4 3 2
      ♣ 4 2

Bid 1 ♠. A poor choice, but the least of evils. Your hand isn't strong enough for a no-trump bid, and your hearts are too weak for a penalty pass.

(d)   ♠ 6 4 3
      ♡ K J 9 8
      ◊ K 10 8 6
      ♣ J 4

Bid 1 NT. If your side should have game, it is much more likely to be in notrump than in diamonds, and you are just strong enough for the constructive notrump response.

(e)   ♠ 6 4 3
      ♡ Q 9 5
      ◊ A 4 3
      ♣ Q J 9 7

Bid 2 ♣. Your hearts probably won't be an adequate stopper opposite partner's promised shortness, and only an incurable optimist would evaluate this poorly distributed mess of queens and jacks as worth a 9-point jump response.

(f)   ♠ K Q 8 7
      ♡ 6 5 2
      ◊ A 6 5 2
      ♣ 7 3

Bid 2 ♠. Jump to show a hand worth 9-11 points.

(g)   ♠ 6 5 3
      ♡ 7 6 5 2
      ◊ A K 3
      ♣ K 10 9

Bid 3 ◊. An awkward situation, but there is no better choice.

(h) ♠ A Q J 2   *Bid* 2 ♡. Game is probable,
     ♡ 7 6 3 2   especially since none of your
     ◇ 7   values are wasted in hearts, so
     ♣ K Q 8 7   cue-bid to show at least 12
                             points. If partner now bids
                             2 ♠, jump directly to 4 ♠.

(i) ♠ 7   *Pass.* Allowing partner's dou-
     ♡ K Q J 10 6 2   ble to stand commands a
     ◇ 6 4 2   trump lead from partner. The
     ♣ Q 5 2   opponents are likely to be in
                             serious trouble—*if* you draw
                             their trumps before they can
                             score some tricks by ruffing.

RESPONDING AFTER INTERFERENCE

If your right-hand opponent inserts a bid over your
partner's takeout double, you can add two additional weapons
to your bidding arsenal:

1. *Pass.* You are relieved of the obligation to speak, so pass
with an undistinguished hand.

2. *The responsive double.* In an auction like

YOU	LHO	PARTNER	RHO
—	1 ♡	Double	2 ♡
?			

many experts play that a double now is *responsive,* showing a
hand like

          ♠ K J 3
          ♡ 6 5 4 2
          ◇ A 10 7
          ♣ K 3 2

The responsive double says: "Partner, I've got useful values—at least 10 points—but I don't have any good four-card or longer suits and I can't bid notrump because I don't have any stoppers in the opponents' suit. It looks like we have the balance of strength, so I can't afford to pass, but it's up to you to decide what we should do." The responsive double is useful for hands that are difficult to bid by any other method, and it gives up very little because you will rarely (if ever) want to double for penalties on this particular auction.

Let's return to our previous examples, this time supposing that your right-hand opponent has bid 2 ♡ over your partner's takeout double.

YOU	LHO	PARTNER	RHO
—	1 ♡	Double	2 ♡
?			

(a)　♠　J 9 7 6
　　　♡　6 3 2
　　　◊　A 10 8 7 2
　　　♣　5

Bid 2 ♠. This nonjump two-level response shows about 6-8 useful points. Pass

(b)　♠　5
　　　♡　6 3 2
　　　◊　A 10 8 7 2
　　　♣　J 9 7 6

Pass. Partner will act again if his hand is very strong.

(c)　♠　J 9 7
　　　♡　Q 10 9 3 2
　　　◊　4 3 2
　　　♣　4 2

Pass. You're not strong enough for a double even if you play that it is for penalties. The opponents might well make 2 ♡; or partner may pull the double with his probable heart void and go for a million opposite your collection of junk.

(d) ♠ 6 4 3
     ♡ K J 9 8
     ◇ K 10 8 6
     ♣ J 4

Pass. Your heart strength figures to be wasted in a diamond contract, and you're not strong enough for a bid of 2 NT.

(e) ♠ 6 4 3
     ♡ Q 9 5
     ◇ A 4 3
     ♣ Q J 9 7

Pass. Your heart queen will probably be useless on offense, your distribution is awful, and much of your points are in lowly queens and jacks.

(f) ♠ K Q 8 7
     ♡ 6 5 2
     ◇ A 6 5 2
     ♣ 7 3

Bid 3 ♠. Jump to show 9-11 points.

(g) ♠ 6 5 3
     ♡ 7 6 5 2
     ◇ A K 3
     ♣ K 10 9

Double (responsive). Shows good values but no clear idea as to what to do.

(h) ♠ A Q J 2
     ♡ 7 6 3 2
     ◇ 7
     ♣ K Q 8 7

Bid 3 ♡. A 4 ♠ response is reasonable, but would tend to show longer spades and less high-card strength.

(i) ♠ 7
     ♡ K Q J 10 6 2
     ◇ 6 4 2
     ♣ Q 5 2

Pass. Even if you play that a double is for penalties, partner will surely pull it with his heart void. Hope that he re-opens with a second double, in which case you will happily pass for penalties. (And check the deck after the deal is over to be sure that it doesn't have fifteen hearts!)

Suppose instead that the auction proceeds:

YOU	LHO	PARTNER	RHO
—	1 ♡	Double	Redouble
?			

Let partner know if you have a decided preference among the unbid suits, but pass with an indifferent hand. For example:

(a)	♠ 6 5 3	(b)	♠ 8 7	(c)	♠ K Q 8 2
	♡ 7 5 3		♡ 7 5 3		♡ 7 5 3 2
	◇ 6 4 2		◇ 8 6 2		◇ 6 4
	♣ J 9 7 5		♣ K J 8 6 4		♣ 8 3 2

Pass	Bid 2 ♣	Bid 1 ♠

High cards in your bid suit are even more important than length, for partner may well wind up on opening lead. He will have every reason to be annoyed if he trustingly leads away from an honor in the suit you bid, only to wind up blowing a trick because you've got five to a nine-spot.

Responding When Partner Passes and Then Doubles

Suppose the auction proceeds as follows:

YOU	LHO	PARTNER	RHO
—	1 ♠	Pass	1 NT
Pass	2 ◇	Double	Pass
?			

Partner's delayed double shows a good takeout double of diamonds and a strong hand. Bid 2 ♡ with

♠ 6 3
♥ J 8 7 5
♦ J 4 3
♣ 10 9 8 6

However, suppose you hold:

♠ 3
♥ Q 9 8 5 2
♦ 7 6 3 2
♣ A 6 4

You are worth a nonforcing game invitation of 3 ♥, which partner will be happy to accept by bidding 4 ♥ with a hand like

♠ A 10 8 7
♥ A K 10 6
♦ A
♣ J 7 5 2

Finally, special action is necessary holding:

♠ K J 9 6
♥ 5 2
♦ 7 6 4 3
♣ 6 4 3

Your best spot should be in spades, even though the opponents have bid the suit, so bid 2 ♠ — a signoff, not a cue-bid.

BALANCING AUCTIONS

If partner passes originally and then makes a balancing double or overcall, remember that he is expecting you to have useful values because the enemy bidding has died at a low level. For example:

YOU	LHO	PARTNER	RHO
—	1 ♡	Pass	2 ♡
Pass	Pass	Double	Pass
?			

You hold:

♠ A 7 3 2
♡ J 9 5
◇ 7 4 3
♣ A Q 2

Don't let your high-card strength lure you into making a jump response; a bid of 2 ♠ is quite sufficient. Partner's hand:

♠ K 8 6 5
♡ 7
◇ Q 9 6 2
♣ K 10 8 3

Responding to an Overcall

PREEMPTIVE OVERCALLS

Respond to a preemptive overcall by your partner just as you would to a preemptive opening bid. For example (only the opponents are vulnerable):

YOU	LHO	PARTNER	RHO
—	1 ◇	3 ♠	Pass
?			

(a) ♠   4
     ♡   A 7 6 2
     ◇   A K 5 4 3
     ♣   A 10 8

Bid 4 ♠. Partner has promised six tricks and a superb spade suit, and you can add four tricks. A 3 NT bid would be a bad choice because of your poor fit in spades; partner's preempt denies much side-suit strength, so you're likely to be cut off from dummy's long spade suit if you play in no-trump.

(b) ♠   9 8 7 4
     ♡   K J 8
     ◇   6 3
     ♣   A 8 6 5

Bid 4 ♠. The vulnerable opponents should be cold for a game in a red suit, so help blockade the auction. A 4 ♠ sacrifice should be worthwhile even if doubled.

(c) ♠   A 9 6 4
     ♡   A K 6
     ◇   Q J 10
     ♣   Q J 10

Bid 3 NT. If partner has a typical 3 ♠ bid such as seven spades to the K Q and two small cards in each side suit, 3 NT will be cold; but the opponents can cash the first four tricks against a 4 ♠ contract.

(d) ♠   8 6 4
     ♡   Q J 8 7
     ◇   K J 9
     ♣   K Q J

Pass. Side-suit queens and jacks are usually of little value opposite a preemptive bid. Hope to wind up on defense, where they'll do more good.

(e) ♠   8
     ♡   Q 7 3
     ◇   6 3
     ♣   A Q 9 8 7 5 2

Pass. Partner's suit is at least as good as yours, and fighting with him can only enrich the opponents.

WEAK JUMP OVERCALLS

A weak jump overcall shows a preemptive hand that is too weak by one trick to bid at the three-level, so you need somewhat more strength to act than you would after a higher-level preempt. For example, if your left-hand opponent opens the bidding with 1 ◊, partner overcalls 2 ♠, and the next player passes, you should bid 4 ♠ with

> ♠ K 6
> ♡ 8 5 4
> ◊ A K 10 3
> ♣ A Q 10 4

because you expect to have a good play for it even if partner has as little as six spades to the A Q. You should also bid 4 ♠ holding

> ♠ 10 8 6 4
> ♡ 7
> ◊ 8 6 4
> ♣ A Q 10 6 3

unless you are vulnerable and the opponents are not. They appear to be a cinch for game, and a 4 ♠ sacrifice should be eminently worthwhile — especially if it pushes them one trick too high. But pass with

> ♠ 8 6
> ♡ Q J 8 7
> ◊ A J 9
> ♣ K Q 6 2

You aren't going anywhere opposite a weak jump overcall, and neither are the opponents in view of your defensive strength.

REGULAR OVERCALLS

A regular overcall shows a respectable suit and a decent hand, so your responding strategy is fairly similar to your actions after your partner opens the bidding. The main difference is that you should pass more readily with an unimpressive hand, since partner may have only 9 or 10 points for his overcall. For example, suppose the auction proceeds:

YOU	LHO	PARTNER	RHO
—	1 ♣	1 ♠	Pass
?			

You should act as follows:

Response to Overcall	*Meaning*
Single raise to 2 ♠	7-10 points; three-card or longer spade support.
Double raise to 3 ♠	11-13 points; good three-card or longer spade support.*
Triple raise to 4 ♠	Strong offensive, distributional hand; excellent spade support.
Nonjump in new suit	*Not* constructive; good suit, fair hand, poor support for partner's suit. Partner needs a strong hand to bid again.

*A good alternative is to use the *jump* cue-bid (in this case, 3 ♣) – an otherwise wasted call—to show 11-13 points and good support. This permits you to use the double raise (here, to 3 ♠) as a preempt, showing a hand like

♠ Q 7 6 5 3
♡ 6
◇ 7 2
♣ J 8 7 4 2

Jump in new suit	Strong suit; good hand; forcing for one round.
1 NT	8-10 high-card points; good stoppers in enemy suit; balanced hand.
2 NT	11-13 high-card points; good stoppers in enemy suit; balanced hand.
Cue-bid of enemy suit	Powerful hand; asks partner to define his strength. With less than 12 points, he rebids his suit; with 12 or more points, he bids a new suit, notrump, or jumps in his first suit.

Observe that a single raise on a weak 4-6 point collection is *not* recommended. Such a bid is very likely to confuse partner as to your offensive prospects, and it isn't preemptive enough to cause the opponents much trouble.

Let's look at some examples:

YOU	LHO	PARTNER	RHO
—	1 ♣	1 ♠	Pass
?			

(a) ♠ 8 6
    ♡ 6 4 2
    ◊ A Q 9 7 3
    ♣ 8 5 3

Pass. Don't confuse the issue (and risk a sizable penalty) by bidding diamonds.

(b) ♠ K 6 3
    ♡ J 10 4
    ◊ 6 5 4 3
    ♣ Q J 2

Pass. Your distribution is terrible and most of your points are in queens and jacks, so warn partner against competing further.

(c) ♠ K 9 8
♥ 6 3
♦ A 6 5 3
♣ 7 4 3 2

Bid 2 ♠. These values are indeed useful, so encourage partner to fight on.

(d) ♠ Q J 3 2
♥ A Q 9 5
♦ 10 8 7 3
♣ 7

Bid 3 ♠ (or 3 ♣ if you prefer that method), showing 11-13 points and good spade support and inviting partner to continue on to game.

(e) ♠ K 9 8 7 6
♥ 7 2
♦ A Q 9 6 3
♣ 4

Bid 4 ♠. This should finish off the opponents and get you to a good contract.

(f) ♠ 7
♥ K Q 10 8 7 3
♦ Q 6 3
♣ 8 4 2

Bid 2 ♥. Try to improve the contract when your spade support is so poor and your own suit is this strong. Partner is *not* encouraged to bid again, although he may do so with a strong hand.

(g) ♠ Q 6
♥ 8 6 5
♦ J 10 4 2
♣ A Q 9 8

Bid 1 NT. Your club stoppers are excellent, and the partial spade fit will be very useful in a notrump contract.

(h) ♠ —
♥ 8 6 5
♦ Q J 10 6 3 2
♣ K Q 9 8

Bid 2 ♦. Don't play in notrump with terrible support for partner's suit, or with sketchy high-card values. Your bid warns partner not to return to 2 ♠.

(i) ♠ K 7
     ♡ A K 6 5
     ◊ K 10 8 5
     ♣ 7 6 2

Bid 2 ♣. If partner now bids 2 ♠, showing a minimum overcall, pass and take your part-score. If instead he promises at least 12 points by bidding 2 ♡, 2 NT, or 3 ♠ raise directly to game; and if he bids 2 ◊, raise to 3 ◊ (non-forcing).

SUPER-STRONG OVERCALLS

Keep in mind that if partner makes a takeout double and then jumps in a suit, he is showing a super-strong overcall of 19 or more points. Thus, suppose the auction proceeds:

YOU	LHO	PARTNER	RHO
–	1 ◊	Double	Pass
2 ♣	Pass	3 ♠	Pass
?			

Go on to 4 ♠ if you hold

        ♠ Q 6 2
        ♡ 7 4
        ◊ 10 9 3 2
        ♣ A 6 4 2

A queen in partner's suit and a side ace should be enough to produce game. However, pass with a ghastly mess like

        ♠ 8 6 3
        ♡ 6 4 2
        ◊ J 5 3
        ♣ Q 9 7 3

WHEN PARTNER OVERCALLS
AND THEN DOUBLES

As we have seen, an overcall followed by a takeout double shows a good suit, some interest in the unbid suits, and a good hand. For example:

YOU	LHO	PARTNER	RHO
—	1 ♡	1 ♠	2 ♡
Pass	Pass	Double	Pass
?			

Return to 2 ♠ with a hand like

♠ 8 6 3
♡ 7 4 2
◇ K J 5 3
♣ 10 6 2

Partner is more interested in three-card spade support than a four-card minor suit. (If his preferences were the other way around, he would have started with a takeout double.) However, bid 3 ◇ with

♠ 8 2
♡ 7 6 4
◇ K J 10 7 5
♣ 10 6 3

And with

♠ 8
♡ 7 6 4 2
◇ A K 9 7 5
♣ K 4 2

you should invite game by jumping to 4 ◊ (nonforcing). A direct bid of 3 ◊ over 2 ♡ would have been bad strategy, for your singleton in partner's suit might well have portended a catastrophic misfit. But now that he has shown some support for the unbid suits, you can safely get into the act. Finally, pass for penalties if you happen to have a hand like

♠ 8
♡ Q J 10 9
◊ A 7 4 3
♣ 10 9 3 2

With your impressive trumps, side ace, and spade shortness combined with partner's strong hand, the opponents should find that even a two-level contract can be very expensive!

NOTRUMP OVERCALLS

After a 1 NT overcall by your partner, use a 2 ♣ response as the usual (and invaluable) Stayman Convention, asking partner to bid a four-card major suit if he has one and to bid 2 ◊ if he does not. Some players use a cue-bid of the enemy suit as Stayman, but this can get the auction rather high in a hurry—especially if the opening bid was in spades. A nonjump response in a new suit is a signoff; a jump in a new suit is forcing to game; and notrump raises retain the usual meaning. For example:

YOU	LHO	PARTNER	RHO
—	1 ◊	1 NT	Pass
?			

(a) ♠ 7 6 3
    ♡ Q 9 4 2
    ◊ 6 5 3
    ♣ K 5 3

Pass. Partner's bid shows 16-18 points, so you aren't going anywhere.

(b) ♠ K J 10 3
    ♡ A 10 9 7
    ◇ 6 3
    ♣ 5 4 2

Bid 2 ♣ (Stayman). If partner shows a four-card major suit, raise directly to game. If instead he bids 2 ◇, invite game by bidding 2 NT; your doubleton diamond won't be an asset in a notrump contract, so allow partner to pass with a 16-point minimum.

(c) ♠ K J 8 6 5
    ♡ 7 6 3
    ◇ 8
    ♣ 10 9 4 2

Bid 2 ♠. Partner must pass.

(d) ♠ A Q 10 6 3
    ♡ K 6 5
    ◇ 7
    ♣ 10 9 4 2

Bid 3 ♠. This is forcing to game, and asks partner to choose between 3 NT and 4 ♠ depending on the quality of his spade support.

Responding to a Cue-Bid

If you elect to try one of the following cue-bids, be sure to discuss matters in advance with your partner in order to avoid a costly bidding misunderstanding.

MICHAELS CUE-BID

After a Michaels Cue-Bid, it is usually best to respond in one of the cue-bidder's long suits. For example:

YOU	LHO	PARTNER	RHO
—	1 ♣	2 ♣*	Pass
?			

*Michaels Cue-Bid

(a) ♠ 9 5 3
   ♥ 7 2
   ♦ A Q 10 8 3
   ♣ 7 4 2

Bid 2 ♠. Partner has promised at least 5-5 in the major suits.

(b) ♠ J 10 7 3
   ♥ Q 6
   ♦ 7 4 3 2
   ♣ A 5 3

Bid 3 ♠. This invites partner to go on to game with a maximum. Your secondary high cards are well placed in partner's suits, and your side-suit value represents a sure trick.

(c) ♠ A Q
   ♥ J 10 7 3
   ♦ 7 4 3
   ♣ A 6 5 3

Bid 4 ♥. Game should be there for the taking.

(d) ♠ J 10 7 3
   ♥ Q 10 6 5 3
   ♦ 7
   ♣ 8 5 2

Bid 4 ♥. The *opponents* should have game for the taking, so jam their auction before they wake up. Your distribution ensures that a 4 ♥ sacrifice, even if doubled, will be worthwhile.

(e) ♠ 8 7
   ♥ 9 2
   ♦ K Q 10 8
   ♣ K Q J 8 2

Bid 2 ♥. Be as conservative as possible. Your high cards will be mostly wasted opposite partner's shortness, and no-trump contracts on misfits are usually disastrous.

If instead partner cue-bids in a major suit, you won't know for certain which minor he has. However, to play in his minor, you can simply bid clubs; partner will convert to diamonds if that is his second suit.

ASTRO CUE-BID

After an Astro Cue-Bid, responder's top priority is to show four or more cards in the major suit promised by the cue-bidder. Failing this, responder usually returns to the cue-bidder's long minor. Some examples:

YOU	LHO	PARTNER	RHO
—	1 ♣	2 ♣*	Pass
?		*Astro Cue-Bid	

(a) ♠ K Q 6 2
    ♡ J 8 7 2
    ◇ 7 3
    ♣ 5 4 2

Bid 2 ♡. Partner's Astro Cue-Bid shows four hearts and six diamonds.

(b) ♠ 7 6 3
    ♡ A K 7 5
    ◇ Q 8
    ♣ 10 9 4 3

Bid 4 ♡. All partner needs for you to have game is four hearts to the queen and six diamonds to the A K, which would be a rock-bottom minimum cue-bid.

(c) ♠ J 7 6 2
    ♡ 7 3
    ◇ Q 6
    ♣ Q J 10 7 2

Bid 2 ◇. Partner has promised a very strong diamond suit. Your bid recommends that he leave the rest of the bidding, if any, to the opponents.

ROTH CUE-BID

A Roth Cue-Bid shows a very strong takeout double, so you should respond by bidding a good side suit — preferably a four-card or longer major suit. Partner has promised at least 19 points, so you need only about 5 points to invite game by jumping in a new suit. Similarly, a bid of 2 NT shows only 3-5 high-card points, stoppers in the enemy suit, and a balanced hand; a bid of 3 NT is similar but shows 6-9 high-card points; and a cue-bid of the enemy suit shows at least 7 points and is forcing to game.

A final observation: Except perhaps for once-in-a-lifetime situations (such as nine cards in the suit partner has cue-bid), you should never pass any of these cue-bids by your partner!

Rebids by the Takeout Doubler: A Technical Note

Discussing every auction that could possibly follow a takeout double would be hopelessly tedious; fortunately, it is also unnecessary. So long as you have a clear understanding of the meaning of the various responses that partner can make, you should have little trouble deducing the best way in which to follow up your takeout double. Thus, there is little need to move back across the table into the doubler's chair and spend a great deal of time discussing the choices at your second turn to bid.

There is one rebidding situation that does confuse many players, however; it concerns the cue-bid response. For example:

YOU	LHO	PARTNER	RHO
—	—	—	1 ♡
Double	Pass	2 ♡	Pass
?			

It is obvious that passing 2 ♡ would be distinctly bizarre, but how long are you forced to bid? Must you continue the auction until game is reached, or is there some way to stop in a part-score?

The recommended procedure is to treat the auction after a cue-bid response to a takeout double as *forcing until one player makes a minimal bid,* such as a single raise of partner's suit or a simple rebid of a suit bid previously. (The force is also removed, of course, if game is reached.) For example:

YOU	LHO	PARTNER	RHO
—	—	—	1 ♡
Double	Pass	2 ♡	Pass
2 ♠	Pass	3 ♠	Pass
?			

Partner's single raise of your suit is a minimal bid and therefore shows only about 12 or 13 points, the least that you could expect him to have for his cue-bid. (With more, he would either jump directly to 4 ♠ or make a forcing bid.) Thus, you should pass if you have a minimum takeout double and can see that your side will be short of the 26 points needed to bid game.

Here's another example:

YOU	LHO	PARTNER	RHO
—	—	—	1 ♡
Double	Pass	2 ♡	Pass
2 ♠	Pass	3 ◇	Pass
?			

Partner has bid a new suit, so you are forced to continue the auction. If you have a minimum hand and don't mind if partner stops below game, you can bid 3 ♠ or 4 ◇. But if you have extra strength and want to make certain that game is reached, you must either bid it directly or make a forcing bid such as 3 ♡ or 4 ♣.

COMPETING IN SECOND POSITION

Review Quiz

Part I.

In each of the following problems, your right-hand opponent's opening bid is shown. Plan your competitive strategy, including your second bid where appropriate.

(1)
RHO opens 1 ♣
♠ K Q 10 6
♡ A Q 10 5
◇ A Q 8
♣ 7 3

(2)
RHO opens 1 ♡
♠ Q 6 5 3
♡ 7
◇ A 10 6 3
♣ J 8 3 2

(3)
RHO opens 1 ♡
♠ K J 6
♡ A Q 8
◇ K 10 4 3
♣ K J 9

(4)
RHO opens 1 ◇
♠ A Q 6 2
♡ 6
◇ A 10 4 3
♣ A J 10 2

(5)
RHO opens 1 ♠
♠ 7
♡ A J 6
◇ K Q 10 8 3 2
♣ K J 7

(6)
RHO opens 1 ♠
♠ 7
♡ 5 4 2
◇ A Q J 9 7 6
♣ K 10 8

(7)
RHO opens 1 ◇
♠ A 8 3 2
♡ K Q 10 5
◇ 7.
♣ K 10 6 2

(8)
RHO opens 1 ♡
♠ A 10 7
♡ 6 3 2
◇ J 7
♣ A Q 9 6 5

(9)
RHO opens 1 ♣
♠ A Q
♡ A K Q 8 6
◇ A J 10 7
♣ 8 2

(10)
RHO opens 1 ♣
♠ 7
♡ A Q J 9 6 3
◇ J 10 2
♣ 9 8 3

(11)
RHO opens 1 ◇
♠ A K J 8
♡ 7 2
◇ 10 8 3
♣ A Q 10 2

(12)
RHO opens 1 ◇
♠ A Q J 9 7 6 4 3
♡ —
◇ 6 4 2
♣ 8 7

(13)
RHO opens 1 ♠
♠ 6
♡ K Q 10 7
◇ A Q J 6 3 2
♣ 7 2

(14)
RHO opens 1 ♡
♠ —
♡ A Q 9 6 5
◇ K Q J 7 3
♣ A 10 8

(15)
RHO opens 1 ♠
♠ 7
♡ K Q 7 2
◇ K 6 3
♣ A Q J 10 6

(16)
RHO opens 1 ♡
♠ K Q 10 9 5
♡ 7 6
◇ A 6 3
♣ A 10 8

(17)
RHO opens 1 ♡
♠ A Q 6
♡ 8 7 3
◇ A K Q
♣ A 10 7 6

(18)
RHO opens 1 ♠
♠ Q 2
♡ 9 7 2
◇ K Q 10 2
♣ A K 5 3

(19)
RHO opens 1 ◇
♠ A K 10 5
♡ J 7 6 4 3
◇ 6
♣ A J 5

(20)
RHO opens 1 ◇
♠ A J 6 3
♡ A K J 7
◇ —
♣ K J 10 6 2

Part II.

In each of the following problems (except as noted in numbers 28 and 29), the auction proceeds as follows:

YOU	LHO	PARTNER	RHO
—	1 ◇	Double	Pass
?			

What call do you make?

(21)
♠ Q 8 6 3
♡ 4
◇ 7 6 4
♣ K J 9 7 6

(22)
♠ K Q 8 5
♡ 7 6
◇ 6 3 2
♣ A J 10 4

(23)
♠ 6 3 2
♡ 8 7 5
◇ 5 3 2
♣ J 7 5 4

(24)
♠ 9 7 6
♡ 8 7 6
◇ K Q 8 7 6
♣ 7 4

(25)
♠ 10 9 7
♡ 6
◇ K Q J 10 8 6
♣ 5 4 2

(26)
♠ A J 3
♡ Q 10 2
◇ 7 4
♣ A K 6 5 3

(27)
♠ K 6 3
♡ J 10 8 2
◇ K Q 10 7
♣ 5 2

(28) RHO bids 2 ◇
♠ K 9 3
♡ A 10 3
◇ 6 5 3 2
♣ K J 8

(29) RHO bids 3 ◇
♠ A 5 3
♡ K Q 8 2
◇ 7 4 3 2
♣ J 2

Part III.

In each of the following problems, the auction proceeds as follows:

YOU	LHO	PARTNER	RHO
—	1 ◇	1 ♠	Pass
?			

What call do you make?

(30)
♠ 10 8 7 4
♡ A Q 6 4
◇ 6 3
♣ 7 4 2

(31)
♠ J 9 6
♡ J 8 7
◇ Q 6 3
♣ K 5 4 2

(32)
♠ 8
♡ Q J 10 9 7 3
◇ A 4 2
♣ 6 5 3

(33)
♠ 8
♡ A Q 6 4 2
◇ 9 6 3
♣ J 8 7 2

(34)
♠ J 9
♡ A 6 4
◇ K J 10 8
♣ 10 7 4 3

(35)
♠ K 7
♡ A K J 6 3
◇ 8 5 3
♣ Q 10 3

Solutions

1. *Double.* You will make a single raise of any one-level response by partner, showing values markedly in excess of a minimum takeout double. If instead partner jumps to 2 ♡ or 2 ♠, showing 9-11 points, raise directly to game.

2. *Pass.* Your distribution is ideal for a takeout double, but your hand is too weak.

3. *One notrump.* Shows 16-18 high-card points, a balanced hand, and stoppers in the enemy suit.

4. *Pass.* Your distribution is wrong for an immediate takeout double. Hope to be able to make a takeout double on the next round of bidding.

5. *Two diamonds.* A good *six*-card suit takes priority over only *three*-card support for an unbid major. If partner remains silent and a good opportunity arises, you will make a takeout double on your next turn to bid.

6. *Two diamonds.* This time, you must plan to pass on your next turn unless partner makes a forcing bid, for you are not strong enough to take additional action on your own.

7. *Double.* An ideal pattern. Your strength is minimal for a takeout double, however, so you must pass a nonjump response by partner. If instead be bids 2 ♡ or 2 ♠, make one more try for game by raising to the three-level; and if he cue-bids 2 ◇, bid 2 ♡ and make sure that game is reached on your next turn to bid.

8. *Pass.* Don't overcall at the two-level with such a weak suit.

9. *Double.* You will next jump in hearts to show a "super-strong" heart overcall worth 19 or more points.

10. *Two hearts.* A typical weak jump overcall — a strong six-card suit and little defensive strength.

11. *One spade.* One of the rare instances where an overcall in a four-card suit is justified. You have a strong hand and a strong suit that you can bid at the one-level, and your bid blocks out a 1 ♡ response by your left-hand opponent.

12. *Four spades.* A typical preemptive overcall.

13. *Double.* You can convert a club response to diamonds without increasing the level of bidding, so look for a 4-4 major-suit fit. If instead your long minor were in clubs, you would have to increase the level of bidding to convert to your long suit, so a 2 ♣ overcall (or Astro Cue-Bid) would be preferable.

14. *Pass.* Stay out of the auction on the first round with such length in the enemy suit. You may well be able to make a more descriptive takeout double of spades later on — or a killing penalty double if (as seems likely) the hand is a misfit for both sides.

15. *Double.* You can stand any response by partner, so seek out a 4-4 major-suit fit. You are strong enough to compete further in clubs at your second turn if the opponents' bidding dies in 2 ♠.

16. *One spade.* Locating a 5-3 spade fit is the top priority. If an enemy 2 ♡ bid is passed back to you, you can then double for takeout to show your secondary interest in the minor suits; but if the auction is higher than that at your next turn, pass.

17. *Double.* You're too strong to pass. Your extra

strength will make up for your lackluster distribution.

18. *Pass.* Your support for the unbid major is weak, and the spade queen is likely to be useless for offensive purposes.

19. *Double.* Treat the weak five-card heart suit like a four-carder.

20. *Double.* If partner responds 1 ♡, 1 ♠, or 2 ♣, show your great strength by making a double raise. If instead your left-hand opponent competes with 2 ◊ or 3 ◊ and this is passed back to you, you are strong enough to compete further by making a second takeout double.

21. *One spade.* Do your share to help find an invaluable 4-4 major-suit fit by giving the four-card spade suit priority over the five-card minor.

22. *Two spades.* Jump to show 9-11 points and to invite game. A 1 ♠ response could be made on a Yarborough.

23. *Two clubs.* Don't panic and pass! Partner must allow for an abomination like this one.

24. *One heart.* Least of evils. Your diamonds aren't nearly strong enough for a penalty pass, your hand isn't strong enough for a constructive 1 NT response, and you don't have a four-card suit to bid, so bid your cheapest three-carder.

25. *Pass.* Your diamond suit is strong enough to draw the opponents' trumps, and the pass demands a trump lead from your partner. If declarer is prevented from gaining tricks by ruffing, your side should rack up a profitable penalty.

26. *Two diamonds.* Cue-bid to show that you have at least 12 points. You can bid clubs next time.

27. *One notrump.* A constructive bid, showing about 7-10 high-card points, a balanced hand, and good stoppers in the enemy suit.

28. *Double (responsive).* The responsive double shows important high-card values, but no clear idea what to do—no good suit to bid and no stoppers in the opponents' suit for notrump purposes.

29. *Three hearts.* Ordinarily, you would jump to show 9-11 points, but you cannot commit your side to game with only 10 points. Partner should realize that you have useful values since you acted freely at the three-level.

30. *Two spades.* You have good spade support and a few useful high cards.

31. *Pass.* A raise would show a willingness to fight for the contract if the opponents compete further, and the last thing you want with this uninspiring collection is for partner to bid again.

32. *Two hearts.* Strongly suggests that partner pass, although he may bid again with a powerful hand. If he raises to 3 ♡, accept his invitation and go on to 4 ♡.

33. *Pass.* Partner's heart support may be as bad as your spade support. Don't risk a substantial penalty by fighting with him; he's on your side.

34. *One notrump.* Shows 8-10 high-card points, good stoppers in the enemy suit, and a balanced hand with a mild fit with partner's suit.

35. *Two diamonds.* Find out how strong partner is. If he bids 2 ♠, showing less than 12 points, pass and settle for a part-score. If he does anything else, showing at least 12 points, bid hearts as cheaply as possible (forcing) to ask him to help select the best game contract. If he then bids 3 ♠, showing a six-card spade suit, raise to 4 ♠; if he bids 4 ♡ or 3 NT, pass.

2

Competing in Fourth Position

♠ ♡ ◇ ♣

In bridge, as in politics, "left" and "right" have quite different implications. If your *right*-hand opponent deals and opens the bidding with one of a suit, a judicious entry into the auction could easily result into a bonanza for your side. Partner, after all, has not yet been heard from, so he may well have useful values that will enable you to make a part-score, a game, or even a slam. However, if your *left*-hand opponent is the culprit who has dealt and opened with one of a suit and your partner has passed, an entry into the auction could easily result in a catastrophic disaster. Unless partner is trapping or planning a delayed action, his silence augurs ill for your chances, especially if your right-hand opponent gangs up on you by joining in the auction.

Competing After Both Opponents Have Bid

TAKEOUT DOUBLES

There are good reasons to be conservative after an auction like

YOU	LHO	PARTNER	RHO
–	1 ♡	Pass	1 ♠
?			

Both opponents are bidding and partner is maintaining a discreet silence, so entering the auction with a shaky takeout double is likely to have disastrous consequences. Also, the opponents are likely to buy the contract, so a bid by you, *even if safe,* may give away vital information. For example (both sides vulnerable):

NORTH
♠ A 10 5 3
♡ K 8 7
♢ 6 5 4
♣ 6 3 2

WEST
♠ Q 9 8 2
♡ Q 6 5 4
♢ Q 7
♣ 7 5 4

EAST
♠ J 6 4
♡ —
♢ A K J 10 8
♣ K J 10 9 8

SOUTH
♠ K 7
♡ A J 10 9 3 2
♢ 9 3 2
♣ A Q

SOUTH	WEST	NORTH	EAST
1 ♡	Pass	1 ♠	Double
Pass	2 ♣	Pass	Pass
3 ♡	Pass	4 ♡	Pass
Pass	Pass		

East's takeout double was reasonably "safe" in view of his strength, but it nevertheless proved fatal for his side. Upon hearing that the missing minor-suit strength was marked in East's hand, South perked up, promoted his club queen in value, and bid aggressively to game. West led the queen of diamonds, and East cashed three diamond tricks and cleverly

played a fourth round of the suit. Under ordinary circumstances, South might well have discarded his queen of clubs and
ruffed in dummy, preferring to stake his contract on one finesse
rather than two, and conceded defeat when West then turned
up with a trump trick. Conditions, however, were far from
normal! Paying close attention to the road map provided by
East's takeout double, South rose to the occasion by making a
star play: He trumped the diamond in his hand and immediately
finessed the jack of hearts through West. The rest was easy.
South picked up the remaining trumps with the aid of a second
finesse, then took the marked club hook to bring home his
contract. Lucky? Of course — but East deserved his bad luck,
for his double was wrong on several counts:

1. East could hardly expect to hit the jackpot by bidding
and making a game. Both of his suits were minors, so he would
have to take eleven tricks against two bidding opponents to
score the lucrative game bonus.
2. Even a part-score was unlikely, for the opponents
would probably outbid him in one of the higher-ranking major
suits.
3. An eventual sacrifice did not figure to be worthwhile in
view of the vulnerability.
4. North's forcing 1 ♠ response ensured that the auction
would continue for a while, so East could compete later on if
the opponents stopped at a low level after finding a fit.

As you can see, even sufficient strength does not necessarily justify a takeout double in fourth position after both
opponents have bid. If, however, you can enter the auction with
reasonable safety *and with a fairly good chance of buying the
contract,* you should do so. Trying to stop opponents from
converting part-scores has caused sharp booms in aspirin stocks,
and it is far better to saddle them with the headaches by making
the partial yourself. In addition, if you are not vulnerable and
the opponents are, competing may well allow you to find a
worthwhile sacrifice against an eventual game contract by the
enemy. Let's look at some examples:

Auction 1.

YOU	LHO	PARTNER	RHO
—	1 ♡	Pass	2 ♡
?			

To make a takeout double on this auction, you need a solid opening bid with fine support for all unbid suits, such as

♠ K 10 6 3
♡ 7
◇ K Q 8 7
♣ A 10 9 5

There is some hazard in competing at the two-level in this situation, for your left-hand opponent just might be happily contemplating a 22-point powerhouse. But the risk must be taken. Partner should have a few cards in the enemy suit in view of your shortness, so he is unlikely to balance if 2 ♡ is passed around to him even when it is your hand; and your side is likely to have a good suit fit because the opponents have found one of their own.

With either of the following hands, a pass is preferable:

(a) ♠ Q 9 6 3   (b) ♠ 8 6 3
    ♡ 7   ♡ 7 2
    ◇ Q J 8 7   ◇ K Q 8 7
    ♣ A 10 9 5   ♣ A K 10 2

With hand (a), you're too weak to compete at the two-level; and hand (b) has a vital weakness in the unbid major suit as well as imperfect distribution. It is often wise to let discretion be the better part of valor in fourth position, especially when your distribution is less than ideal.

Auction 2.

YOU	LHO	PARTNER	RHO
—	1 ♣	Pass	1 ♡
?			

On this auction, the opponents have not yet found a fit, making it less likely that your side has one somewhere. On the other hand, partner can bid the unbid major at the one-level in response to a takeout double, and you may be able to make the opponents' life miserable by competing in the highest ranking spade suit. Therefore, it is reasonable to double with

```
♠  A Q 3 2
♡  7
♦  K J 10 8 6
♣  9 8 5
```

if you are not vulnerable, although it would not be wrong to insist on a somewhat more powerful hand like

```
♠  A Q 3 2
♡  7
♦  A Q 10 8 7
♣  9 8 5
```

A pass is best, however, with hands like the following:

(a)
```
♠  K 7 3
♡  A 9 4
♦  A K 6
♣  5 4 3 2
```

(b)
```
♠  Q 7 6 2
♡  A
♦  Q J 6 5 2
♣  K J 3
```

A takeout double would be a poor choice with hand (a) because of the abysmal distribution. Hand (b) suffers from a different problem—too much strength in the enemy suits. The opponents' high cards have to be somewhere; so if you are strong in their suits, they're probably strong in yours—and eager to make a penalty double if you stick your neck out.

Auction 3.

YOU	LHO	PARTNER	RHO
—	1 ◇	Pass	1 ♠
?			

This auction is less auspicious than the preceding one, for two reasons. First, partner will have to bid a suit at the *two*-level in response to a takeout double, which might turn out to be fatal if he is very weak. Second, even if you're lucky enough to find that the strength on the deal is approximately evenly divided, the opponents are likely to outbid you because they own the spades. For example, if each side can make eight tricks in its own major suit, the opponents will win the battle for the part-score by bidding 2 ♠ over your 2 ♡, and you'll have gained nothing by your risky entry into the auction. Therefore, pass (and keep the opponents in the dark as to your distribution) with

♠ 7
♡ A Q 3 2
◇ 5 4 3
♣ K J 10 4 3

To double, you need a stronger hand, such as

♠ 7
♡ A Q 10 6
◇ 5 3 2
♣ A K J 9 8

You should also double with

♠ K 7 5 3
♡ A K J 6
◇ 5
♣ A 7 4 2

You have impressive values and excellent support for the unbid suits. A story goes with this hand, for a mad scientist sitting on your right has inserted a sneaky psychic bid; but skillful competitive bidding by your side will save the day. The complete deal (both sides vulnerable):

NORTH (your partner)
♠ A Q 9 8 2
♡ Q 7
◇ 9 6
♣ 8 6 5 3

WEST
♠ J 6 4
♡ 8 2
◇ A K 7 2
♣ K Q J 10

EAST (the mad scientist)
♠ 10
♡ 10 9 5 4 3
◇ Q J 10 8 4 3
♣ 9

SOUTH (you)
♠ K 7 5 3
♡ A K J 6
◇ 5
♣ A 7 4 2

SOUTH	WEST	NORTH	EAST
—	1 ◇	Pass	1 ♠ (!)
Double	Pass	Pass	3 ◇
3 ♠	Pass	4 ♠	Pass
Pass	Pass		

North passes your double in order to play for penalties, forcing East to show his true colors by escaping to diamonds. Since partner's penalty pass is in effect a spade bid, you now "support" him by bidding 3 ♠, whereupon the spade game is quickly reached—and made with an overtrick.

Auction 4.

YOU	LHO	PARTNER	RHO
—	1 ♡	Pass	1 ♠
?			

This auction is even worse for you than Auction 3, for the opponents have announced possession of both major suits. An immediate takeout double may work out well if you have a very strong minor two-suiter such as

♠ 7
♡ 4 3
◇ A K J 9 7
♣ A K 10 9 5

The opponents are unlikely to be headed for game when you're this strong, so revealing your hand shouldn't cost very much, and bidding now may well avoid a tough decision later on. Usually, however, your best strategy will be to pass and see how the auction develops. If the opponents stop at a low level after finding a fit (for example, when LHO raises to 2 ♠ and RHO passes), you can balance at that point if your hand warrants. If the opponents are unable to reach any agreement (for example, if LHO bids 2 ♡ and RHO passes), you're probably best off out of the auction.

Auction 5.

YOU	LHO	PARTNER	RHO
—	1 ♡	Pass	1 NT
?			

This is the worst auction yet against which to compete, since the 1 NT response warns of a possible misfit. A double shows a good takeout double of hearts and a very strong hand like

        ♠ K 10 8 3
        ♡ 7
        ◊ K 10 9 3
        ♣ A K J 2

Most of the time, however, a pass will be your best choice after an auction like this one.

Auction 6.

YOU	LHO	PARTNER	RHO
—	1 ♡	Pass	2 ♣
?			

This auction is even less promising than Auction 5. The two-over-one response shows at least 10 points, so the opponents are off to the races and your side is clearly outgunned. A takeout double is all too likely either to help the enemy declarer play the hand, or to result in a substantial penalty. Aside from exceptional cases, such as

♠ Q 10 9 6 5
♡ —
◇ A J 10 8 6 2
♣ 7 3

when you are not vulnerable and the opponents are, you should pass. There's always the next deal!

To sum up:

Positive signs suggesting that a fourth-position takeout double may well strike oil include:
1. The opponents have found a suit fit.
2. The opponents have *not* bid spades.
3. Partner can respond at a low level of bidding.
4. You are not vulnerable and the opponents are. (This will be disadvantageous if your side has game, but it makes a devastating penalty double by the opponents less likely—and a worthwhile sacrifice against their eventual game contract more likely.)

Negative signs indicating that you should have second thoughts about doubling include:
1. The opponents have *not* found a suit fit.
2. The opponents have bid spades.
3. Partner must respond at a high level of bidding.
4. You are vulnerable and the opponents are not. (A game for your side will be worth more, but the opponents are much more likely to find a killing penalty double.)

Prohibitive signs that make a pass preferable to a takeout double include:
1. A hand of dubious strength.
2. Imperfect distribution, particularly a hand that lacks four-card or longer support for an unbid major.

3.   Responder has made a strong bid, such as a two-over-one response or a strong jump raise of opener's suit.

4.   The opponents have bid both major suits and, insofar as you can tell from your strength, are likely to be on their way to game.

OVERCALLS

The meaning of overcalls does not change substantially in fourth position, so a brief comment should suffice.

Preemptive overcalls, and weak jump overcalls that can be made at the two-level, are much the same as those made in second position. The sole difference is that a bit more conservatism is in order, for the opponents have already exchanged a round of information and the preempt therefore has less to gain.

Regular overcalls should be somewhat stronger than in second position, especially if the auction is one of the less favorable ones on which to compete. In particular, a strong suit is essential. The opponents may well miss a good penalty double when each one can take three tricks is a side suit, but few adversaries will neglect to double when holding three or four trump tricks.

You're unlikely to hold a super-strong overcall in fourth position against two bidding opponents. If this rare bird does fly into view, doubling and then making a further show of strength (such as bidding your suit, or cue-bidding the enemy suit) should adequately describe your strength.

Finally, imperfect overcalls against two bidding opponents are reserved strictly for those with incurable suicidal tendencies.

RESPONDER'S ACTIONS

Responding to a fourth-position takeout double or overcall is not very different from the procedures described in the preceding chapter, so brevity should be sufficient here also.

If partner has doubled, give the usual top priority to

mentioning an unbid major suit, jump if you see a chance for game and want partner to bid it if he has extra values, cue-bid if you are strong enough to insist on game but aren't sure where to play it, and jump directly to game with a strong major suit and a strong hand. You will not go far wrong if you retain the usual ranges of 0-8 points for a non-jump response, 9-11 points for a jump, and 12 or more points for a cue-bid, although it will pay to shade the latter two requirements slightly if partner shows a strong hand by doubling in an unfavorable auction.

If partner overcalls instead, don't try to improve the contract by changing suits even if your support for his suit is very weak. Overcalls in fourth position promise a strong suit, and you didn't have anything you deemed worthy of mention on your first turn to bid. Thus, you should almost always leave well enough alone.

Balancing in Fourth Position

Competing is difficult when you are outnumbered by two bidding opponents. The fight is much more even, however, after an auction like the following one:

YOU	LHO	PARTNER	RHO
—	1 ◇	Pass	Pass
?			

Here, your right-hand opponent has sadly announced a very weak hand, which tends to cancel out the bad news provided by your left-hand opponent. Even if your own hand isn't particularly impressive, partner may well have trapped on the first round of bidding with a good hand and strength in the enemy suit, so it's often a good idea to compete in auctions like this one.

Surprisingly, various and sundry experts have great difficulty in this apparently simple situation, and frequently wind up in horrendous contracts. (Documentation, in the form of actual examples, will be given later on in this chapter.) To be sure, most would agree that after the above auction, you should balance with a double if you hold

(a) ♠ K 8 7 3
    ♡ Q 10 4 2
    ◇ 6
    ♣ A J 7 2

and overcall with 1 ♡ if you hold

(b) ♠ 7 3 2
    ♡ A Q 9 7 6
    ◇ 6 3
    ♣ Q J 2

Standard methods, however, dictate an initial double with

(c) ♠ 9 3
    ♡ A K 7 4 2
    ◇ J
    ♣ A Q 10 9 2

in order to differentiate it from a weaker holding like hand (b). As we saw in the Prologue, this procedure is likely to lead to serious trouble, for partner will expect a distribution like hand (a) and may therefore bid an unpleasantly large number of spades.

Fortunately, light has recently appeared in this dark area of bidding theory. *Bridge World* editor Edgar Kaplan has suggested that you can use most of your usual competitive bidding methods when balancing in fourth position. This approach has two important advantages: Its effectiveness is satisfactory, and it does *not* require you to spend hours of tedious memorization preparing new methods for a situation that doesn't come up very often.

OVERCALLS

Overcalls in balance position retain the usual meaning. For example (neither side vulnerable):

YOU	LHO	PARTNER	RHO
—	1 ♡	Pass	Pass
?			

(a) ♠ A J 10 9 6 2   *Bid* 2 ♠. A typical two-level
    ♡ 6 2   weak jump overcall.
    ◊ Q 6 3
    ♣ 4 3

(b) ♠ A K 9 7 3   *Bid* 1 ♠. A strong regular
    ♡ 7 4 3   overcall.
    ◊ A Q J 7
    ♣ 9

(c) ♠ A Q 9 7 3   *Bid* 1 ♠. A minimum regular
    ♡ 10 5 2   overcall.
    ◊ K 9 4
    ♣ 8 7

(d) ♠ 2   *Bid* 2 ◊. A regular two-level
    ♡ A 6 2   overcall—with an ace to spare.
    ◊ A J 10 6 4 3
    ♣ A Q 2

(e) ♠ A K Q 8 7 6   *Double.* Then jump in spades
    ♡ 7 3   next time. A typical super-
    ◊ A J 9   strong overcall.
    ♣ K 10

(f)   ♠   A K Q J 7 4
      ♡   A Q 8
      ◇   J 8
      ♣   A 5

Double. Then cue-bid the ene-my suit, and then show your spades. This hand is appre-ciably stronger than hand (e), so urge partner to bid game even with as little as the king of hearts and out.

TAKEOUT DOUBLES

A balancing double in fourth position promises the usual ideal or imperfect distribution, so partner can confidently respond in any unbid suit at whatever level his strength dictates. It's a good idea to use a two-step strategy based on your general strength:

Strength	*Procedure*
10-13 points	Double; then pass a nonjump new-suit bid by partner. If he invites game by jumping, accept with 12 or 13 points but pass with only 10 or 11 points.
14-16 points	Double; then make one more try for game by raising a nonjump new-suit bid by partner. If instead he invites game, accept.
17 or more points	Double; then cue-bid the enemy suit.

Some examples:

YOU	LHO	PARTNER	RHO
—	1 ♡	Pass	Pass
?			

(a) ♠ K 9 7 6
    ♡ 7
    ◇ A 10 6 2
    ♣ 10 9 7 3

Double. You have a minimum, so pass any non-forcing response by partner.

(b) ♠ K 9 7 6
    ♡ 7
    ◇ A 10 6 2
    ♣ Q J 10 3

Double. Pass any nonjump bid by partner. If instead he invites game by bidding 2 ♠, go on to 4 ♠.

(c) ♠ K J 7 6
    ♡ 7
    ◇ A Q 6 2
    ♣ K 10 4 3

Double. If partner makes a nonjump bid in a new suit, try once more for game by making a single raise.

(d) ♠ K J 7 6
    ♡ 7
    ◇ A K Q 6
    ♣ K 10 4 3

Double. Follow with a cue-bid of the enemy suit to show a very powerful hand.

(e) ♠ Q 10 8 5
    ♡ 5 3
    ◇ A Q 9 8
    ♣ J 9 7

Double. A typical "imperfect" takeout double.

(f) ♠ K 9 7 6
    ♡ 7
    ◇ Q J 6 2
    ♣ 8 7 5 3

Pass. You're too weak to bid, and (as we saw in Chapter 1) partner's pass shows a maximum of 16 points. You may miss a part-score, but such a loss on occasion will hardly be ruinous.

(g)   ♠   7 3
       ♡   K 9 7 6
       ◇   A 10 6 2
       ♣   Q 9 7

Pass. You're weak in the unbid major, and your length in hearts makes it unlikely that partner is trapping.

BALANCED HANDS

The only competitive bid that takes on a new meaning when you are balancing in fourth position is the bid of 1 NT. This bid shows 8-12 high-card points and a balanced hand, and it does *not* promise any stoppers at all in the enemy suit. It conveys the following message to your partner:

"Partner, I'm bidding in order to protect you in case you trap-passed on the first round with a good hand and strength in the suit bid by the opponents. *If you didn't trap pass, we don't have game, and we may not have enough stoppers in the enemy suit to play in notrump.* After all, if *I* had length and strength in the opponent's suit, I'd know that you probably weren't trapping, so I'd *pass* with this mediocre collection. Therefore, if *you* don't have the enemy suit stopped, *it may well be a good idea to escape to a good side suit—even a strong four-carder.* If, however, you *did* trap pass with strength in the enemy suit, notrump should be a good spot. If game is possible opposite my 8-12 points, let me know by raising notrump, and I'll carry on to 3 NT with an 11- or 12-point maximum."

It may seem paradoxical to bid notrump without stoppers in the enemy suit; since this is the only unusual aspect of balancing in the fourth position, let's review the reasoning. If you have length and strength in the suit bid by the opponents, partner probably doesn't. Therefore, he is probably *not* trapping, so there's no need for you to protect him by balancing with an inferior hand. If, however, you are short in the enemy suit, partner is more likely to be long and strong in it and more likely to have trapped on the first round of bidding. Therefore, you should balance even if your hand is flat and only about average in strength, and the 1 NT bid is reserved for this purpose.

With 13-16 high-card points and a balanced hand, double first and then bid notrump over partner's response. (This is the only time when you may double with only two-card support for an unbid suit.) If you have 17-19 points, bid 2 NT. Some examples:

YOU	LHO	PARTNER	RHO
—	1 ♡	Pass	Pass
?			

(a)   ♠   K J 3
     ♡   7 2
     ◇   K J 10 6 3
     ♣   7 6 2

Bid 1 NT. You're not strong enough for a regular two-level overcall. Your bid doesn't promise any heart stoppers; if you didn't think partner was trapping with heart strength, you wouldn't bid at all.

(b)   ♠   7
     ♡   Q J 8 7
     ◇   J 8 7 3
     ♣   K Q 3 2

Pass. Because of your heart length, you can surmise that partner probably isn't trapping, and you have a mediocre hand with shortness in the unbid major.

(c)   ♠   J 8 7 6 2
     ♡   7 3 2
     ◇   A Q 6
     ♣   K 2

Bid 1 NT. Your spades aren't strong enough for a regular overcall.

(d) ♠ K 7
     ♡ Q J 8
     ◇ K Q 6 3
     ♣ K 10 6 2

Double. You will bid notrump over partner's response, showing 13-16 high-card points and a balanced hand.

(e) ♠ K 3
     ♡ Q J 2
     ◇ A Q 8 7
     ♣ A Q 6 2

Bid 2 NT. This shows 17-19 high-card points and a balanced hand.

CUE-BIDS

If you have decided to use the Michaels, Astro, or Roth Cue-Bid in second position, keep things simple by doing the same in the fourth seat. If not, a reasonable alternative is to cue-bid instead of doubling when you have a 5-4-4-0 distribution with the shortness in the enemy suit. The problem with the double is that partner may well be loaded in trumps and elect to pass for penalties, and the defense will suffer because you won't be able to lead even one round of trumps through declarer.

RESPONDER'S ACTIONS

If partner has balanced with a double in fourth position, remember that he may be bidding just to protect you in case you trap passed on the first round. Therefore, don't invite game by jumping the bidding unless you actually were trapping and have a hand that is worth an opening bid.

If instead partner balances with 1 NT, a quick escape may be indicated if you don't have any stoppers in the opponent's suit. For example:

YOU	LHO	PARTNER	RHO
—	—	—	1 ♡
Pass	Pass	1 NT	Pass
?			

If you hold

     ♠   8 6 3
     ♡   7 4
     ◇   A Q 6 3
     ♣   K J 10 8

game is out of reach because partner's 1 NT bid shows at most 12 points, so your goal is to find a makable part-score. Notrump may well be disastrous because partner may not have any heart stoppers, so remove to 2 ♣, allowing partner to bid diamonds cheaply if he doesn't like your first selection. However, it is better to pass with

     ♠   8 6 3
     ♡   7 4 2
     ◇   A Q 6 3
     ♣   K J 7

Your distribution is terrible for suit play, you have only one respectable suit to offer, and your support for the unbid major is weak. Even if the opponents are able to run the first four or five tricks in their suit, a 1 NT contract should be a reasonable spot.

     If you do hold strength in the enemy suit, notrump is probably the best contract. Pass with

     ♠   7 4
     ♡   K J 9
     ◇   A 9 8 5
     ♣   Q J 8 2

Game is unlikely in view of partner's upper limit of 12 points. However, invite game by raising to 2 NT with

$$
\begin{array}{ll}
\spadesuit & \text{K 7} \\
\heartsuit & \text{K J 9} \\
\diamondsuit & \text{A 9 8 5} \\
\clubsuit & \text{Q J 8 2}
\end{array}
$$

Game is easier to make when most of the enemy strength is known to be in one hand (the hand of the opening bidder), so you can afford to be somewhat more aggressive than usual; a combined total of 25 points, or perhaps even 24, may well prove sufficient for game in notrump or a major suit. If partner carries on to 3 NT with an 11-point hand, your side will have "only" 25 points, but you'll be favorites to make your contract. If instead you hold

$$
\begin{array}{ll}
\spadesuit & \text{K Q 9 6} \\
\heartsuit & \text{A 6 3 2} \\
\diamondsuit & \text{7} \\
\clubsuit & \text{K J 10 2}
\end{array}
$$

and wish to determine whether or not partner has four cards in the unbid major, a cue-bid of 2 ♡ will be just what the doctor ordered.

Finally, if partner has balanced with an overcall, the usual responding methods should suffice.

CHALLENGING THE CHAMPS

For the past six years, *The Bridge World* has run a monthly bidding competition between two pairs of experts. Some of the typically difficult deals from "Challenge the Champs" have involved balancing in fourth position, and the results have been so dismal that the moderator recently sent out an SOS. "Clearly," he observed, "this area needs lots of study." These deals offered an opportunity to test out the methods recommended in this chapter against the results of the world's leading experts, and here's how the suggested methods fared:

> Better than the experts: 15 times
> Equally well: 14 times
> Worse than the experts: 2 times
> Uncertain*   6 times

Here are some of the more interesting examples:

> North deals and opens 1 ♠
> East-West vulnerable

WEST		EAST	
♠	A K Q	♠	J 6
♡	A	♡	Q J 9 6 4
◇	8 3	◇	J 9 4 2 .
♣	K Q J 8 5 4 3	♣	10 2

A 3 NT contract might or might not pay off on this unusual deal, depending on the acumen and the holdings of the defenders; but no one would want to be in 5 ♣—least of all the world-famous pair who saw their debacle publicized in *The Bridge World*. If West wishes to gamble, he can bid 3 NT directly when 1 ♠ is passed around to him. If he prefers to bid accurately, he can show his super-strong overcall:

---

*A result was "uncertain" if the outcome depended more on the individual player's judgment than on the bidding methods that were used; if the best contract was unclear; or if the competitors, who were asked to assume that they were playing in a match-pointed pairs contest (where aggressiveness is desirable and minor-suit contracts are usually undesirable), might well have produced saner results under more normal circumstances.

SOUTH	WEST	NORTH	EAST
–	–	1 ♠	Pass
Pass	Double	Pass	2 ♡
Pass	4 ♣	Pass	Pass
Pass			

On the following deal, the recommended methods easily locate a good major-suit fit that was missed by the experts:

North deals; South bids 1 ♠
North-South vulnerable

WEST	EAST
♠ K 6	♠ J 7 3
♡ Q J 9 6 4	♡ K 3 2
◊ A 7 3	◊ K Q 5
♣ J 7 4	♣ K 10 9 6

North deals and passes, East also passes, and South opens the bidding with 1 ♠. West is too weak for a two-level overcall, so he passes, and East balances with 1 NT. Assured that partner has a balanced hand, and hence at least some support for hearts, West signs off in 2 ♡—the best contract. The experts did not fare so well: Both Wests passed the 1 NT balance, fearing it might have been made with shortness in hearts.

Slam is unlikely after an enemy opening bid, but not impossible:

North deals and opens 1 ♠
North-South vulnerable

WEST	EAST
♠ 2	♠ 9 8 5 3
♡ A K Q 2	♡ 6
◊ A 10 5	◊ K 9 8
♣ K J 8 6 4	♣ A Q 5 3 2

One expert pair gathered its courage and bid bravely to 5 ♣! The other pair reached the laydown club slam. The recommended auction is:

SOUTH	WEST	NORTH	EAST
–	–	1 ♠	Pass
Pass	Double	Pass	2 ♣ (a)
Pass	2 ♠ (b)	Pass	4 ♣ (c)
Pass	4 NT (d)	Pass	5 ◇ (e)
Pass	6 ♣ (f)	Pass	Pass
Pass			

(a) "I wasn't trapping on the first round; I've got less than an opening bid. Sorry!"

(b) "That's O.K. *I've* got at least 17 points."

(c) "Well, in that case, you'll be glad to know that my club suit is pretty good, and I've got some values outside of spades where they're likely to be some help."

(d) "How many aces?"

(e) "One."

(f) "That's all I need to know!"

On the following deal, a well-known expert missed a laydown game.

North deals and opens 1 ◇
East-West vulnerable

WEST	EAST
♠ A K Q J 7 4	♠ 10 9 5
♡ A Q 8	♡ J 6 4 2
◇ J 8	◇ 10 4 3
♣ A 5	♣ K 6 2

The recommended auction is:

SOUTH	WEST	NORTH	EAST
–	–	1 ◇	Pass
Pass	Double	Pass	1 ♡
Pass	2 ◇	Pass	2 ♡
Pass	3 ♠	Pass	4 ♠
Pass	Pass	Pass	

The expert West also balanced with a double but followed '
with a jump to 2 ♠, and East took a quick look at that
gruesome collection and couldn't pass fast enough.

The silliest result of all was the 4 ♠ contract reached by
an expert pair on the following deal:

> South deals and opens 1 ♡
> Both sides vulnerable

WEST	EAST
♠ A Q 4	♠ K J 5
♡ 10 7 6 3	♡ 5
◇ 8 3	◇ A K 10 9 7 5 2
♣ A Q 7 2	♣ 8 4

Their auction (?) went as follows:

SOUTH	WEST	NORTH	EAST
1 ♡	Pass	Pass	3 ◇
Pass	3 ♡	Pass	3 ♠
Pass	4 ♣	Pass	4 ◇
Pass	4 ♠	Pass	Pass
Pass			

If you can explain that bidding, I'll be happy to forward your analysis to the experts in question (who obviously need all the help they can get). Here's a saner suggestion:

SOUTH	WEST	NORTH	EAST
1 ♡	Pass	Pass	2 ◇
Pass	2 ♡	Pass	4 ◇
Pass	5 ◇	Pass	Pass
Pass			

East shows a regular two-level overcall in diamonds, and West tries for game by cue-bidding to ask East to define his strength. East, justly proud of his seven-card suit, shows extra values (but no heart stoppers) by jumping to 4 ◇, so West bids the game in diamonds.

No bidding procedure works well on all hands (else there would not be disagreement as to what to use), so you may get an occasional bad result using the suggested methods. Most of the time, however, your balancing auctions will be as effective, or more so, than those of the experts — and what could be more enjoyable than that?

Review Quiz

Part I.

In each of the following problems, the vulnerability and bidding are as shown. What call do you make?

(1)   Neither side vulnerable

LHO	PARTNER	RHO	YOU
1 ♡	Pass	2 ♡	?

You hold:

♠ Q 8 6 2
♡ 6
◇ A K 10 7
♣ A 9 8 5

(2)   Neither side vulnerable

LHO	PARTNER	RHO	YOU
1 ◇	Pass	1 ♠	?

You hold:
- ♠ 6
- ♡ K 9 8 5
- ◇ Q 8 7 4
- ♣ A Q 10 8

(3)   You are vulnerable

LHO	PARTNER	RHO	YOU
1 ♠	Pass	2 ♠	?

You hold:
- ♠ 6
- ♡ Q J 3 2
- ◇ A 10 7 2
- ♣ K J 6 3

(4)   Neither side vulnerable

LHO	PARTNER	RHO	YOU
1 ◇	Pass	1 ♡	?

You hold:
- ♠ Q 9 5
- ♡ 6 2
- ◇ K 9 6 5
- ♣ A K J 8

(5)   Both sides vulnerable

LHO	PARTNER	RHO	YOU
1 ♣	Pass	1 ◇	?

You hold:
- ♠ A Q J 9 7
- ♡ K 10 8
- ◇ 7
- ♣ 6 4 3 2

(6)   Both sides vulnerable

LHO	PARTNER	RHO	YOU
1 ♣	Pass	1 ♠	?

You hold:
♠ 7
♡ A Q J 9 7
◇ K 10 8
♣ 6 4 3 2

(7)   Neither side vulnerable

LHO	PARTNER	RHO	YOU
1 ♠	Pass	2 ◇	?

You hold:
♠ 7 5
♡ A Q 8 6 5
◇ 4
♣ K Q 9 7 6

(8)   Both sides vulnerable

LHO	PARTNER	RHO	YOU
1 ♣	Pass	1 ◇	?

You hold:
♠ 10 9 8 7 3
♡ K Q 8 6
◇ 3
♣ A K 2

(9)   Both sides vulnerable

LHO	PARTNER	RHO	YOU
1 ♡	Pass	2 ♡	?

You hold:
♠ Q 7 6 2
♡ 7
◇ A J 10 7
♣ 7 6 5 3

(10) Both sides vulnerable

LHO	PARTNER	RHO	YOU	You hold:
1 ♣	Pass	1 ♡	?	♠ Q 10 7 6
				♡ 5
				◇ A J 8 7 2
				♣ A 9 3

(11) Both sides vulnerable

LHO	PARTNER	RHO	YOU	You hold:
1 ♡	Pass	1 ♠	?	♠ 7 3
				♡ 6
				◇ A Q J 6 2
				♣ A J 10 9 4

(12) Opponents are vulnerable

LHO	PARTNER	RHO	YOU	You hold:
1 ♠	Pass	1 NT	?	♠ A 3
				♡ K Q J 6
				◇ 8 7 5 2
				♣ Q J 10

Part II.

In each of the following problems, the auction proceeds as follows:

YOU	LHO	PARTNER	RHO
—	1 ◇	Pass	Pass

Unless otherwise indicated, neither side is vulnerable. What call do you make?

(13)
♠ A Q 8 6
♡ J 10 8 3
◇ 3 2
♣ Q 10 3

(14)
♠ 7
♡ K Q 9 5 3
◇ 5 3 2
♣ A K Q 4

(15)
♠ A J 8 6
♡ J 3
◇ 7 6 2
♣ K Q 8 5

(16)
♠ 7
♡ Q J 3
◇ K 8 4 2
♣ Q 9 7 6 3

(17)
♠ K Q J 9 7 6
♡ 7 3
◇ 6 4 2
♣ 10 9

(18)
♠ A 10 6 3
♡ J 10 4 2
◇ ——
♣ K 8 6 4 2

(19)
♠ 2
♡ A K Q 8 7 3
◇ A Q 5
♣ Q 10 9

(20)
♠ K 4 3 2
♡ Q 5
◇ 10 3 2
♣ Q 8 7 5

(21)
♠ 6 5
♡ 4 2
◇ A 7 3
♣ A Q J 7 6 3

(22)
♠ K Q 8 6
♡ A Q 7 5
◇ 7
♣ Q J 10 7

(23)
♠ A Q 4 2
♡ K 3
◇ K 10 7
♣ Q 10 3 2

(24)
♠ K J 10 7
♡ A K Q 5
◇ 6
♣ K J 8 4

(25)
Both sides vulnerable
♠ A 3
♡ 6 4
◇ K J 10 8 4
♣ A K Q 10

Solutions

1. *Double.* You have a solid opening bid with fine support for all unbid suits, and your side may well own the all-important spade suit.
2. *Pass.* RHO's bid is forcing, so there is no need to act immediately. If LHO raises to 2 ♠ and this is passed back to you, you can balance with a double; if the opponents fail to find a fit, you're well off out of the auction. Your strength is modest, and the opponents own the spades.
3. *Pass.* A double might work out well, but there are several ominous signs. The opponents have the spades; the vulnerability is unfavorable; partner will have to bid at the three-level; and your strength is only moderate. A double would not be unreasonable at match points, but don't risk a huge set at rubber bridge to try for a doubtful part-score.
4. *Pass.* Your distribution is uninspiring. To add to the general gloom, the king of diamonds is in front of the diamond bidder and may turn out to be wasted.
5. *One spade.* You have the key requirement for an overcall—a strong suit. You may be able to outbid the enemy in spades, direct a favorable opening lead against their eventual contract, or bother LHO by preventing him from making a cheap heart rebid.
6. *Pass.* You're not strong enough for a *two*-level overcall.
7. *Pass.* Gas stations give out free road maps, but there is no reason why you should be equally generous. RHO's two-over-one response shows at least 10 points and the opponents have bid spades, so you're very unlikely to buy the contract. Thus, a double is all too likely to help the enemy declarer play his contract.
8. *Double.* You have a good hand and good support for the unbid suits, and the spade suit is too weak for an overcall. Although the opponents haven't found a fit,

partner can respond at a very low level, and *both* majors are unbid.

9. *Pass.* You're too weak to have much chance of buying the contract unless partner can act on his own.

10. *Double.* A diamond overcall would be wrong on two counts: The suit is too weak, and finding a spade fit is more important.

11. *Pass.* The auction isn't over. If LHO raises to 2 ♠ and this is passed back to you, you'll be much better placed to compete.

12. *Pass.* The 1 NT response strongly suggests a misfit, so remain on the sidelines unless you have ideal takeout double distribution of the enemy suit and a strong hand.

13. *Double.* A minimum "imperfect" double. Pass any nonforcing response by partner.

14. *One heart.* Shows a regular overcall, so there is no need to double and thereby risk an awkward jump response in spades.

15. *One notrump.* If partner now bids 2 ♣, pass; he wasn't trapping, sees no hope for game, and has poor diamond stoppers. If instead he invites game by bidding 2 NT, go on to 3 NT; and if he cue-bids 2 ◇, bid 2 ♠.

16. *Pass.* You're much too weak for a two-level overcall. It's a good idea to avoid the 1 NT bid with shortness in an unbid major, especially since your diamond length makes it unlikely that partner was trapping. Besides, your hand isn't balanced.

17. *Two spades.* A typical weak jump overcall. Using the same methods in second and fourth position avoids headaches.

18. *Double.* If partner bids 1 ♡, 1 ♠, or 2 ♣, pass. If instead he invites game by jumping to 2 ♡ or 2 ♠, accept.

19. *Double.* You will jump in hearts next to show a super-strong overcall. Change the club queen to the

ace, however, and you should double, cue-bid diamonds, and then bid hearts, for partner is undoubtedly looking at a horrendous mess and will need very strong inducement to bid game even when it is cold.

20. *Pass.* You're too weak for a bid of 1 NT. Missing a partial once in a while is no disgrace!

21. *Two clubs.* A typical two-level overcall.

22. *Double.* If partner bids a new suit without jumping, try for game by making a single raise. If instead he invites game by jumping the bidding, accept.

23. *Double.* You will bid notrump next to show 13-16 high-card points and a balanced hand.

24. *Double.* You will cue-bid diamonds on the next round to show 17 or more points.

25. *Pass.* A double would be for takeout. Perhaps your side can make 3 NT, but why confuse the issue? The opponents are vulnerable, so even an undoubled penalty should be satisfactory.

3

Reopening and Negative Doubles

♠ ♡ ◇ ♣

Opponents, like most people, enjoy getting in on a good thing. When they see you overcome their opening bids by using takeout doubles and overcalls to reach excellent partials and games, they will try and return the injury by competing when your side opens the bidding. When they do, however, you can strike back effectively by using a familiar weapon—the takeout double.

Reopening Doubles

REOPENING AT LOW LEVELS

Suppose the auction proceeds as follows:

YOU	LHO	PARTNER	RHO
1 ♡	2 ♣	Pass	Pass
?			

Your left-hand opponent has tried to wrest the controls from you, but there's no reason he should be allowed to get away with such high-handed tactics. If your hand is strong enough, you can get back in the driver's seat by using techniques similar to those described in the preceding chapters. For example, if you have a strong suit, there is no need to request partner's cooperation in choosing the trump suit, so take matters into your own hands by bidding 2 ♡ with

♠ 7 3
♡ A K J 9 6 5
♢ K Q 10
♣ 5 2

and reopen with 2 ♢ if you hold

♠ 7 2
♡ A Q 8 6 5
♢ K Q 10 9 3
♣ 4

Often, however, you will need to consult with your partner in order to determine the best trump suit for your side. Walking around the table to look at his hand is frowned upon, and it is not even necessary; you can inquire about his best suit by making a reopening double. In the above auction, for example, double with

♠ K J 6 3
♡ A Q 8 4 2
♢ A 10 4
♣ 7

This double is for takeout; it asks partner to bid a four-card or longer suit, preferably a major. If he is unable to oblige, he can return to your first suit. A 2 ♡ rebid by you would be ill-advised for two reasons:

1. Partner might well leave you there with a singleton or even a void in hearts, a possibility too gruesome to contemplate.

2. Partner may well have passed on the first round with a decent spade or diamond suit—even a five-carder—because he lacked the strength needed to respond at the two-level, so involving him in the decision is likely to pay rich dividends.

Actions like these are called *reopening* bids because they start the auction up again in a position where a pass would bring it to a screeching halt.* To reopen with a double, you need about 16 points (less if you elect to use the "negative" double described later in this chapter), strong three-card or better support for the unbid suits, and enough defensive strength to avoid a disaster in the event partner passes for penalties with a smattering of strength in the enemy suit and a high card or two on the side. Don't reopen with a double, however, if the auction proceeds

YOU	LHO	PARTNER	RHO
1 ♡	2 ♣	Pass	Pass
?			

and you hold

      ♠ K 4 3
      ♡ K 9 7 6 4 2
      ◇ K Q 9 6
      ♣ —

Your distribution meets the requirements, but it's a poor idea to give partner a chance to pass for penalties when you have such limited values and a void in the enemy suit. If you wish to compete, bid 2 ◇.

Sometimes a dignified surrender is in order. After the above auction, you should pass with

      ♠ 7 4
      ♡ K J 8 6 5
      ◇ K Q 9
      ♣ K J 8

*The terms "reopening" and "balancing" are frequently used interchangeably. For clarity, "reopening" will refer to situations where your side has opened the bidding, and "balancing" to situations where the enemy has begun the auction.

Your heart suit is weak, aceless hands are unexciting for offensive purposes, and your club strength may well be wasted because it is in front of the overcaller.

Any similarity between the preceding auction and the following ones is primarily coincidental:

	YOU	LHO	PARTNER	RHO
(a)	1 ♡	Pass	1 ♠	2 ♣
	?			
(b)	1 ♡	2 ♣	Pass	3 ♣
	?			
(c)	1 ♡	Pass	Pass	1 ♠
	?			

A double of 2 ♣ in auction (a) is for penalties. There is only one unbid suit, so the easiest and best way to call it to partner's attention would be to bid 2 ◊.

A double in auctions (b) and (c) is for takeout, but don't make it unless you have a very strong hand (say, 18 points or more). In auction (b), partner will have to bid at the three-level in order to show a suit, and the opponents won't need an inordinate amount of courage to double a nine-trick contract. In auction (c), partner has shown a woefully weak hand by passing your opening bid, so your best course will usually be to let well enough alone. Used judiciously, however, takeout doubles in these situations can produce substantial profits, especially when combined with keen declarer play. Here's an interesting example:

NORTH
- ♠ 10 6 2
- ♡ 8 4
- ♢ 9 8 3 2
- ♣ A J 3 2

WEST
- ♠ 5 4 3
- ♡ 7 2
- ♢ J 6 5
- ♣ 10 8 7 6 4

EAST
- ♠ A K Q J 7
- ♡ K 6 5 3
- ♢ 10 7 4
- ♣ 9

SOUTH
- ♠ 9 8
- ♡ A Q J 10 9
- ♢ A K Q
- ♣ K Q 5

SOUTH	WEST	NORTH	EAST
1 ♡	Pass	Pass	1 ♠
Double	Pass	3 ♣	Pass
4 ♡	Pass	Pass	Double
Pass	Pass	Pass	

South was delighted to get a second chance to show his great strength by making a takeout double of East's 1 ♠ bid; and North, whose 5-point total was the most that could be expected after his initial pass, elected to jump to 3 ♣ to show his "maximum." South then decided that his strong suit would make game in hearts a good risk even though North hadn't promised any support; and East, who could hardly be blamed for his initial balance, showed his annoyance at this unexpected turn of events by making an ill-judged penalty double.

The defenders started off with three rounds of spades, and

South ruffed the third spade and paused to take stock. "Time for a finesse, partner," he announced, and led the queen of hearts from his hand! North blinked in amazement, but this unusual and inspired play was no boon at all for East. If he won with the king of hearts and made the best return of a spade, South would carefully preserve his own trump length by discarding and ruffing with dummy's eight of hearts, reenter his hand, draw trumps, and claim his contract. Therefore, East ducked the heart queen and permitted declarer to win his "finesse."

South would now go down if he played another round of trumps from his hand. East would win and lead another spade, forcing South to fatally reduce his trump length by ruffing. (Dummy, now out of trumps, could no longer help out in this regard.) South, however, was equal to the occasion. He led a low club to dummy's jack and played the eight of hearts, putting in the jack when East played low. South then cashed the ace of hearts and played off all his minor-suit winners; East could ruff with his high trump whenever he liked, but the contract was safely home.

North deserves kudos for turning up with such vitally important cards as the club ace, heart eight, and spade ten,* but most of the applause belongs to South for his impressive declarer play. Had he carelessly banged down the ace of hearts at trick four and followed with the queen, a spade return would have wrecked the contract. It was also tempting to enter dummy twice in clubs in order to try two heart finesses, but this line would have failed when East ruffed the second round of clubs. South realized that East, who had bid spades and also shown length and strength in trumps by making a penalty double, was likely to be short in clubs, which made the

---

*If West has the eight of hearts, East can defeat the contract by capturing the queen of hearts with his king and returning a spade. If South ruffs in his hand, East has a second trump winner by virtue of his length; and if South discards, West tops dummy by ruffing with the heart eight. (Similar reasoning obviously applies if East has the eight of hearts and West has the seven-spot.) If West has the spade ten, the contract can also be beaten; East shifts to his singleton club at trick two, and later leads a low spade to West's ten in order to obtain a club ruff.

spectacular play of the queen of hearts essential in order to
bring home the contract.

REOPENING AT HIGH LEVELS

Enemy preempts can fracture the happiest partnerships.
Here's a sad example of one that created havoc by inducing
North to make a misguided reopening double (North-South
vulnerable):

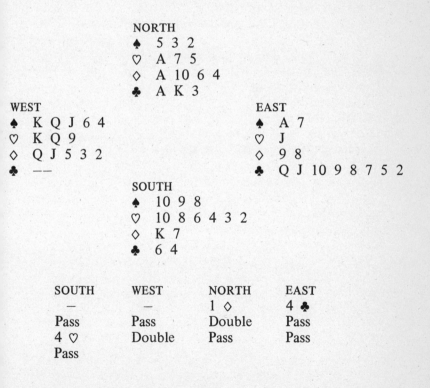

```
                    NORTH
                    ♠  5 3 2
                    ♡  A 7 5
                    ◇  A 10 6 4
                    ♣  A K 3
WEST                                    EAST
♠  K Q J 6 4                            ♠  A 7
♡  K Q 9                                ♡  J
◇  Q J 5 3 2                            ◇  9 8
♣  --                                   ♣  Q J 10 9 8 7 5 2
                    SOUTH
                    ♠  10 9 8
                    ♡  10 8 6 4 3 2
                    ◇  K 7
                    ♣  6 4
```

SOUTH	WEST	NORTH	EAST
—	—	1 ◇	4 ♣
Pass	Pass	Double	Pass
4 ♡	Double	Pass	Pass
Pass			

West led the king of spades, East overtook with the ace
and returned a spade, and West cashed two more spade tricks
and continued with a fourth round of the suit. Ordinarily,
giving declarer a ruff and discard is disastrous, but South did

not appreciate West's apparent generosity. Ruffing with dummy's ace of hearts would guarantee the defenders three trump tricks, and discarding from dummy produced the same result when East ruffed with the jack of hearts. Down 800!

"Look, clod," North complained. "I had 4 ♣ beat in my own hand! What do you mean by bidding with such cheese?"

"What do *you* mean by doubling with such junk?" South shot back. "Your double says that we're likely to have game if I have a long suit and a bit of high-card strength. You should have passed, instead of encouraging me to commit hara-kiri, and been content with an undoubled penalty!"

Some experts would side with North, but South had the better argument. North's double had relatively little to gain, for he was unlikely to register more than a two-trick set, and it would cost a great deal if East turned up with a void in one of the red suits and was able to make his contract. Furthermore, the reopening double in an auction like this one is needed for a more important purpose—namely, locating the best trump suit when game is likely to be a good bet for North and South. Here's how the deal would have gone had North held a hand that truly justified his reopening double:

NORTH
♠ K Q J 3
♡ A J 7 5
◇ A J 10 9 6
♣ —

WEST
♠ A 7 6
♡ K Q
◇ Q 8 5 3
♣ J 9 3 2

EAST
♠ 5 4 2
♡ 9
◇ 4 2
♣ A K Q 10 8 7 5

SOUTH
♠ 10 9 8
♡ 10 8 6 4 3 2
◇ K 7
♣ 6 4

Here, 4 ♡ is made in comfort (in fact, with an overtrick), and North-South rack up a vulnerable game. Alternatively, West may choose to sacrifice in 5 ♣, but he will gain little by doing so; good defense will collect 500 points, and if instead North and South go on to 5 ♡, they'll make it. The moral: After a high-level preempt, reopen with a double only if you have a strong hand with shortness in the enemy suit and think that your side may have game; with no great desire for partner to bid, pass and be happy with an undoubled penalty.

RESPONDER'S ACTIONS

Suppose the auction proceeds as follows:

YOU	LHO	PARTNER	RHO
–	–	1 ♡	2 ♣
Pass	Pass	Double	Pass
?			

Take the most conservative possible course by returning to 2 ♡ if you have a motley collection like

> ♠ 10 8 4 3
> ♡ J 10 8
> ◇ K 6 5
> ♣ 6 3 2

Partner would need a strong two-bid to make game opposite this mess and your heart support is tolerable, so don't give him even mild encouragement by bidding the weak spade suit. However, a bid of 2 ♠ is eminently correct with

> ♠ Q 10 8 5
> ♡ 7 3
> ◇ K J 5
> ♣ 9 6 3 2

because your spade suit is respectable and your heart support is
poor. And you should invite game by jumping to 3 ♠ with

$$
\begin{array}{ll}
♠ & A \ Q \ 9 \ 7 \ 5 \\
♡ & 9 \ 7 \\
◇ & K \ 5 \ 3 \\
♣ & J \ 6 \ 3
\end{array}
$$

You were almost worth an immediate spade bid on the previous
round, so let partner know that game is very likely.

If you have passed partner's opening bid on the first
round, you need even less strength to make a jump response to
a reopening double:

YOU	LHO	PARTNER	RHO
—	—	1 ♠	Pass
Pass	2 ◇	Double	Pass
?			

You hold:

$$
\begin{array}{ll}
♠ & 6 \\
♡ & 10 \ 9 \ 8 \ 7 \ 3 \\
◇ & 5 \ 4 \ 3 \\
♣ & K \ 10 \ 6 \ 4
\end{array}
$$

A jump bid with such a weak hand may appear suicidal,
but your correct call is 3 ♡! Partner has heard your original
pass, which showed at most 5 points, yet he wants you to bid;
and you have a *five*-card heart suit, a king, and a potential
ruffing value in spades. Partner's hand turns out to be

$$
\begin{array}{ll}
♠ & A \ K \ 9 \ 7 \ 4 \\
♡ & K \ Q \ J \ 2 \\
◇ & 6 \\
♣ & A \ 8 \ 5
\end{array}
$$

and he will happily raise your 3 ♡ response to the excellent contract of 4 ♡. If you erroneously respond only 2 ♡, he will have no choice but to pass, because you might have a Yarborough like

♠ 5 3 2
♡ 8 7 6 5 3
◇ 7 5
♣ 9 6 4

After a high-level reopening double, you can pass more readily with a weak balanced hand; you don't need many tricks to defeat the contract, and partner has promised considerable strength. For example:

YOU	LHO	PARTNER	RHO
—	—	1 ◇	4 ♣
Pass	Pass	Double	Pass
?			

Pass if you hold

♠ J 5 2
♡ K 3 2
◇ 9 7 3
♣ 8 6 4 3

With

♠ 8 5
♡ 10 8
◇ 8 7 4 3 2
♣ 8 6 4 3

a pass might well be disastrous, for your length in diamonds suggests that partner's strength in the suit he has bid will fall

victim to enemy ruffs. Therefore, a bid of 4 ◊ is indicated. And
if you have

> ♠ 8 5
> ♡ 10 8
> ◊ K Q 7 4 3
> ♣ 8 6 4 3

a jump to 5 ◊ should prove highly rewarding, for partner has
promised a strong hand like

> ♠ K Q J 3
> ♡ A J 7 5
> ◊ A J 10 9 6
> ♣ —

Finally, as we have seen, a bid of 4 ♡ is best if you hold

> ♠ 10 9 8
> ♡ 10 8 6 4 3 2
> ◊ K 7
> ♣ 6 4

The Negative Double

When bridge was in its infancy, a double of an opening bid
of one of a suit was used for *penalties*, not for takeout; it
showed a hand with great strength in the enemy suit.
Eventually, however, enlightenment dawned, and bridge theorists realized that this procedure was wrong on several counts:

1. Hands suitable for a penalty double came up very
infrequently.

2. Even when the right hand came up, the double often
failed to produce the desired results. Declarer only needed seven
tricks, so he had a fine chance to make his contract; and when
the doubler was really loaded in trumps, one of the other two

players was usually void and ran out to a different contract.

3. Hands in which partner's help was needed in order to pick the best trump suit were very common, so the double was badly needed for a different purpose.

As a result, approximately 99.99 percent of today's bridge players use this double for takeout.

History has a way of repeating itself, and bridge is no exception. In 1957, another traditional penalty double came under attack when Alvin Roth and Tobias Stone recommended that doubles of enemy *overcalls* be used for takeout. They called their invention the *negative double,* and their reasons for advocating it were more or less as follows:

1. Hands suitable for a penalty double came up very infrequently. By 1957, the level of bridge had improved to the point where competent players no longer fell into the trap of making shoddy two-level overcalls.

2. Even when the right hand came up, the double often failed to produce the desired results. When the doubler was really loaded in trumps, one of the other two players was usually void and ran out to a different contract.

3. Hands in which partner's help was needed in order to pick the best trump suit were very common, so the double was badly needed for a different purpose.

4. Using this double for takeout would usually *not* give up the opportunity to score a substantial penalty when the opponents did step out of line.

As you can see, this rationale is similar to the reasons for using the double of an opening bid of one of a suit for takeout, so there is nothing at all mysterious about the negative double. Because it represented such a startling change from traditional methods, however, it met with considerable resistance (and derision) at the outset. In fact, some "experts" (who wouldn't hesitate to make a one-level takeout double) tried to have the negative double banned as unfair, tremendously complicated, and a disservice to the game of bridge! But as time went by, it became apparent that negative doubles have important advantages. The result has been that the majority of today's experts now use them (in fact, 64 percent according to a 1967 *Bridge World* poll).

ADVANTAGES OF NEGATIVE DOUBLES

A few examples will illustrate why negative doubles have become so popular.

YOU	LHO	PARTNER	RHO
—	—	1 ♡	2 ♣

You hold:

♠ K J 8 6
♡ 10 2
◇ A Q 8 7
♣ 6 4 3

Using standard methods, this is an extremely irritating situation! A bid of 2 ◇ or 2 ♠ would seriously overstate your strength, and would promise at least a five-card suit. You can't raise hearts with such poor support. But if you pass, partner may think that you're broke and throw in the towel when your side is cold for a partial—or even a game.

YOU	LHO	PARTNER	RHO
—	—	1 ◇	3 ♠

You hold:

♠ 6
♡ A Q 9 3
◇ 8 6 2
♣ A 10 7 4 3

RHO's preempt is intended to foul up your auction, and he's very likely to succeed if you're using standard methods. You're too weak to bid a new suit, and your diamonds are too weak for a raise. But a pass might well cost you an ice-cold game.

In both of these examples, the negative double is an ideal solution. It asks partner to take out to an unbid four-card or longer suit, preferably a major. If you make a negative double in the first example, partner will bid 2 ♠ with a normal opening bid and four or more spades; you now invite game by raising to 3 ♠, and your auction is back on the right track. If instead partner has a strong opening bid and four or more spades, he'll invite game himself by jumping to 3 ♠, and you'll go on to 4 ♠. Finally, if partner doesn't have good spades and lets you know by making a bid such as 2 ♡, you can pass with the assurance that you are not missing a 4-4 spade fit. Similar reasoning applies in the second example.

DISADVANTAGES OF NEGATIVE DOUBLES

Negative doubles put additional pressure on opener in reopening situations. For example, suppose the auction proceeds

YOU	LHO	PARTNER	RHO
1 ♠	2 ♣	Pass	Pass
?			

and you hold

♠ A Q J 5 3
♡ 7 2
◇ A Q 2
♣ 6 4 3

If you are not playing negative doubles, you should pass. The sounds of partner's silence represent a warning, for he can't have a hand worth an opening bid—or even 7 or more points and good spade support. You own hand is a minimum, so you have little to gain by competing. Using negative doubles, however, you must reopen with a double in order to protect partner in case he is thirsting to penalize 2 ♣. If so, he'll pass, and you'll be in fine shape; but if he has no such idea, he'll have to pull your double, and you may incur a substantial penalty if his hand is very weak.* In practice, this disadvantage has *not* proved serious, but it does represent a potential source of loss when negative doubles are used.

A related problem with negative doubles is that a good penalty may sometimes be missed. For example, if the auction proceeds

YOU	LHO	PARTNER	RHO
1 ◇	2 ♠ *	Pass	Pass
?			

*Weak jump overcall

and you hold:

♠ 6 4
♡ J 8
◇ K Q 10 8 7
♣ A K J 7

you can't afford to reopen with a double because a 3 ♡ response will get you much too high on a possible misfit. Thus, if partner is loaded in spades, he's simply out of luck.

Another possible disadvantage is that you or your partner might have a lapse of memory and forget that a double is negative, which is likely to produce a hideous result. Even experts have been known to commit such a gaffe!

MAKING A NEGATIVE DOUBLE

Negative doubles are used directly over suit overcalls by the enemy. To make a negative double at the one-level or two-level, you need at least 8 points *and* four or more cards in each unbid suit. For example, if partner opens with 1 ♡ and

---

*Your best chance to survive is to pass if he bids 2 ◇ or 2 ♠, and sign off in 2 ♠ if he escapes to 2 ♡.

your right-hand opponent overcalls 2 ♢, a minimum negative double would be

♠ K Q 7 6
♡ 10 3
♢ 6 4 2
♣ K 10 9 6

(Don't count any points for shortness in partner's suit until and unless you find a good trump fit, because you may well wind up playing there!) A negative double is also best with

♠ K Q 7 6
♡ 10 3
♢ 6 4
♣ A 8 6 5 2

A 3 ♣ bid would show a hand worth an opening bid, and finding a spade fit is more likely to land the lucrative game bonus. However, don't make a negative double with either of the following two hands:

YOU	LHO	PARTNER	RHO
—	—	1 ♡	2 ♢

(a) ♠ J 10 3 2   (b) ♠ A K J 7 6
     ♡ J 9 7 6   ♡ 7 3
     ♢ 7   ♢ 9 6 3
     ♣ A 6 4 3   ♣ A 10 4

With hand (a), you have already found one good major-suit fit, and the laws of bridge don't provide any bonus for locating a second trump suit. Keep things simple by adding 2 ♡.

With hand (b), partner probably won't bid a three-card spade suit in response to a negative double, so you need to name your suit in order to locate a 5-3 spade fit. Luckily, you're just strong enough to bid 2 ♠. Change the hand to

> ♠ K J 7 6 3
> ♡ 7 3
> ◇ 9 6
> ♣ A 10 4 3

however, and you should make a negative double; 2 ♠ would be a drastic overbid. And if instead you hold

> ♠ A K J 7 6
> ♡ 7 3
> ◇ 9 6 3
> ♣ 10 4 2

you're still too weak to bid 2 ♠, and a negative double might produce an awkward club response. Pass and hope partner reopens.

Overcoming preemptive overcalls causes difficulty even for experts, so don't be ashamed if a cautious pass results in an occasional loss. To compete, the most common expert practice is to use doubles of three-level overcalls as negative (and promising at least 10 points), but to double for *penalties* if the opponents overcall at the *four*-level or higher. Naturally, it is essential to clarify your understanding with your partner prior to beginning play, and the opponents must also be informed in advance if you are using negative doubles.

RESPONDING TO A NEGATIVE DOUBLE

If partner has made a negative double, respond much as you would to any takeout double; the main difference is that you have the additional option of returning to your first suit. For example, give top priority to a four-card or longer unbid *major,* and invite game by jumping if you have extra values.

After a one-level or two-level negative double, respond as follows:

Your Strength	*Your Choices*
Minimum hand (13-16 points)	Bid new suit without jumping, preferably a major; bid no-trump with stoppers in the enemy suit; rebid first suit without jumping.
Good hand (17-18 points)	Jump in new suit, preferably a major, to invite game (*not* forcing); jump in your first suit (also *not* forcing).
Very good hand (19 points or more)	Jump directly to an indicated game; cue-bid the enemy suit (forcing).

Let's look at some examples. In each instance, partner's double is negative, and both sides are vulnerable.

YOU	LHO	PARTNER	RHO
1 ♠	2 ♣	Double	Pass
?			

(a)
♠ A Q 7 6 3
♡ A 9 6 2
◇ Q 4
♣ 7 3

(b)
♠ A Q J 9 7 6
♡ Q 3
◇ A Q 10
♣ 7 3

(c)
♠ A Q J 9 7 6
♡ K Q 10 5
◇ A
♣ 6 4

With hand (a), bid 2 ♡. Comply with partner's request to mention an unbid (major) suit, but go slow because you have a minimum opening bid and he may have as few as 8 points.

Special action is required on hand (b) in view of your substantial strength. You have no good new suit to bid, so your best procedure is to make a jump rebid of 3 ♠.

Hand (c) is so powerful that game is clearly warranted. However, don't hog the bidding by insisting upon your longest suit! Partner, who is on your team, has promised at least four hearts and may well have only a small singleton spade, so cooperate by bidding 4 ♡.

    (d) ♠ Q 6 5 4 3 (e) ♠ K J 9 6 2
          ♡ K 9 7   ♡ K 7
          ♢ A K J   ♢ A K Q 2
          ♣ 6 3   ♣ 4 3

With hand (d), bid 2 ♢. Your spade suit is too weak to rebid, for partner may well have poor support, and bidding a three-card minor suit that is as strong as this one is most unlikely to cause any serious trouble.

Hand (e) is worth 18 points, and hence a game invitation. Let partner know by jumping to 3 ♢, which also denies possession of four or more hearts.

To pass a low-level negative double, you need long and solid trumps. Your trumps are located in front of declarer, where they can easily be finessed. If declarer needs only seven or eight tricks to make his contract, this unfortunate situation is likely to prove fatal if you defend.

If partner's negative double would require you to bid at the three-level or four-level, you *don't* need powerful trumps to pass. The opponents are probably high enough so that a few tricks in your hand plus partner's promised strength should result in a penalty, so pass if your hand is balanced or if the deal looks like a misfit. However, pull the double if you see a good suit fit somewhere, or if your defensive strength isn't particularly inspiring.

Review Quiz

In each of the following problems, the vulnerability and bidding are shown. What call do you make?

(1)   Both sides vulnerable

YOU	LHO	PARTNER	RHO
1 ♡	2 ◇	Pass	Pass
?			

You hold:
♠ K 6 4 2
♡ A Q J 4 3
◇ 8
♣ A 10 9

(2)   Both sides vulnerable

YOU	LHO	PARTNER	RHO
1 ♡	Pass	Pass	2 ◇
?			

You hold:
♠ K 6 4 2
♡ A Q J 4 3
◇ 8
♣ A 10 9

(3)   Both sides vulnerable

YOU	LHO	PARTNER	RHO
1 ◇	2 ♣	Pass	Pass
?			

You hold:
♠ K Q 10
♡ 6 4 2
◇ A K 6 4 3
♣ 7 6

(4)   Neither side vulnerable

YOU	LHO	PARTNER	RHO	You hold:
1 ♡	2 ◇	Pass	Pass	♠ 7 2
?				♡ K Q J 3 2
				◇ 10 8
				♣ K Q J 9

(5)   Both sides vulnerable

YOU	LHO	PARTNER	RHO	You hold:
1 ♠	2 ♡	Pass	Pass	♠ A Q 10 8 3
?				♡ A Q 9 7
				◇ J 6 5
				♣ 8

(6)   Opponents are vulnerable

YOU	LHO	PARTNER	RHO	You hold:
1 ♠	2 ◇	Pass	Pass	♠ K Q J 8 7 5
?				♡ Q 6 3
				◇ —
				♣ K J 3 2

(7)   You are vulnerable

YOU	LHO	PARTNER	RHO	You hold:
1 ◇	4 ♡	Pass	Pass	♠ A K 6
?				♡ A 4 3
				◇ A 7 6 4
				♣ 6 3 2

(8)   You are vulnerable

YOU	LHO	PARTNER	RHO	You hold:
1 ♠	4 ♡	Pass	Pass	♠ A K J 9 3
?				♡ 3
				◇ A Q J 2
				♣ A 10 9

(9)   Both sides vulnerable

YOU	LHO	PARTNER	ROH	You hold:
—	—	1 ♠	2 ◇	♠ 7 2
?				♡ Q 10 9 3
				◇ A 5
				♣ K 9 6 4 3

(10) Both sides vulnerable

YOU	LHO	PARTNER	RHO	You hold:
—	—	1 ♠	2 ◇	♠ 7 4
?				♡ Q 9 5 3
				◇ 5 4
				♣ · K J 10 6 3

(11) You are vulnerable

YOU	LHO	PARTNER	RHO	You hold:
—	—	1 ♣	1 ♠	♠ 7 3
?				♡ K 10 6 4
				◇ A J 6 5
				♣ 10 4 3

(12) Neither side vulnerable

YOU	LHO	PARTNER	RHO
—	—	1 ♠	2 ♣
?			

You hold:
♠ Q 6 5 3
♡ K 10 9 3
◇ 10 9 8 7
♣ 4

(13) You are vulnerable

YOU	LHO	PARTNER	RHO
—	—	1 ◇	4 ♠
?			

You hold·
♠ Q J 9 7
♡ 7 3 2
◇ 6 5
♣ K 6 4 3

(14) Both sides vulnerable

YOU	LHO	PARTNER	RHO
—	—	1 ♠	2 ◇
?			

You hold:
♠ 7
♡ A 4 3
◇ K J 10 6
♣ 9 8 6 3 2

(15) Neither side vulnerable

YOU	LHO	PARTNER	RHO
1 ♡	2 ◇	Double*	Pass
?			
		*Negative	

You hold:
♠ J 8 4 3
♡ A K 8 6 3
◇ K 10 3
♣ 2

(16) Neither side vulnerable

YOU	LHO	PARTNER	RHO
1 ♠	2 ♣	Double*	Pass
?			
		*Negative	

You hold:
- ♠ A J 10 8 5
- ♡ Q 10 9 7
- ◊ A Q J 9
- ♣ —

(17) Neither side vulnerable

YOU	LHO	PARTNER	RHO
1 ♡	2 ♣	Double*	Pass
?			
		*Negative	

You hold:
- ♠ K 8 3
- ♡ K J 10 7 6
- ◊ Q 3
- ♣ A 5 2

Solutions

1. *Double.* Using standard methods, your side may have game, for partner wouldn't bid freely at the two-level with just four spades to the ace-queen and the king of hearts. Even if he has less, you may well win the part-score battle by outbidding the opponents in a major suit. The answer is the same if you have elected to use negative doubles, but for a different reason. Game is less likely in view of partner's failure to act, but you must protect him in case he wanted to double 2 ◊ for penalties.

2. *Pass.* In this sequence, partner's pass shows at most 5 points, so you need at least 18 points to double.

3. *Pass using standard methods; double if using negative doubles.* Game is unlikely in view of your near-minimum opening bid, so a reopening double is correct only if you are using negative doubles and are therefore obligated to protect your partner.

4. *Pass.* With such meager strength, a pass is best regardless of what methods you are using.

5. *Pass.* This looks like a dangerous misfit. Even if

you're using negative doubles, your length in the enemy suit strongly suggests that partner doesn't need any protection.

6. *Two spades.* Your playing strength warrants one more try, but don't give partner a chance to pass a double for penalties when you have a void in the enemy suit and no aces.

7. *Pass.* A double would strongly encourage partner to bid.

8. *Double.* Game is a strong possibility, and you should defeat 4 ♡ if partner has to pass with a weak balanced hand. In never-never land, where you can bid your partner's hand for him when you feel like it, you could double with Hand 7 and make him pass, and double with Hand 8 and make him bid. In the real world, however, you need his cooperation, and you'll drive him crazy if you double with both Hands 7 and 8. In the long run, you'll win more by reserving the double for hands like this one.

9. *Double (negative).* If partner bids 2 ♠ or 3 ♣, pass; but if he bids 2 ♡, invite game by raising to 3 ♡. If instead *he* invites game by bidding 3 ♡ or 3 ♠, raise to four. (If you're not using negative doubles, isn't it time you started?)

10. *Pass.* Regardless of your methods, you're too weak to bid.

11. *Double (negative).* The negative double makes it easy to find a 4-4 heart fit if you have one.

12. *Two spades.* The simplest course is best even if you're playing negative doubles.

13. *Double.* It is recommended that doubles of four-level overcalls or higher be for penalties.

14. *Double using standard methods; pass if using negative doubles.* Negative doubles probably won't cost you a good penalty, however, for partner will usually reopen with a double (which you will pass).

15. *Two spades.* Shows at least four spades and a minimum opening bid.

16. *Three hearts.* Prefer the unbid major, and jump to invite game.

17. *Two hearts.* No other bid is attractive.

Part **II**.

PENALTY DOUBLES

4

Doubles for Penalties

♠ ♡ ◇ ♣

Truth is reputed to be stranger than fiction, but both can actually be quite remarkable. For example, it might seem that the play of a suit must be automatic and uninteresting when North holds the doubleton K J and East holds the doubleton A Q, but here's a mythical creation from an article of mine in the September 1969 *Bridge World* that proves otherwise:

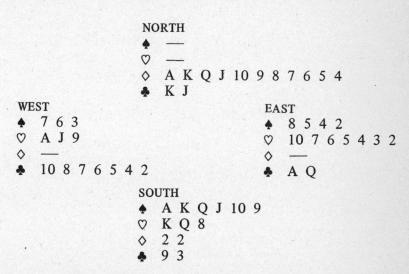

```
                    NORTH
                    ♠  —
                    ♡  —
                    ◇  A K Q J 10 9 8 7 6 5 4
                    ♣  K J
    WEST                                EAST
    ♠  7 6 3                            ♠  8 5 4 2
    ♡  A J 9                            ♡  10 7 6 5 4 3 2
    ◇  —                                ◇  —
    ♣  10 8 7 6 5 4 2                   ♣  A Q
                    SOUTH
                    ♠  A K Q J 10 9
                    ♡  K Q 8
                    ◇  2 2
                    ♣  9 3
```

If North declares the cold game in diamonds, there is no problem (and no story). So let's suppose that South, overly eager to get into the act and score his 150 honors, has opened the bidding out of turn. According to the laws of bridge, the

135

penalty for such a breach of decorum is that the offender's partner is barred from participating in the auction (which, in this case, might well be classified as cruel and unusual punishment). South, forced to act entirely on his own, closes his eyes and bids 4 ♠, and West leads a club. Unlikely as it may seem, the fate of the contract hinges on the play to the first trick! If declarer inserts dummy's jack, East can win the laurel wreath by putting up the *ace* and returning the queen. Dummy is now on lead with a rather restricted choice of plays, and both defenders carefully *discard* on the first round of diamonds. The second diamond is ruffed, however, forever cutting declarer off from dummy's long suit, and South must now lose two heart tricks in addition to the club ace and diamond ruff. On any other defense, declarer wraps up his contract; the defenders can win at most three tricks before South gains the lead, draws trumps, and runs the diamonds. The contract is unbeatable, however, if declarer puts up the *king* of clubs at trick one, because East will now have no way to execute the fatal endplay against the dummy.*

Unusual deals like this one are a delight to fanciers of the outré, but are unlikely to be of much assistance in improving your bridge game. Truth, however, can be almost as strange, especially when the topic of interest is the penalty double.

Winning and Losing Penalty Doubles: Some Illustrative Examples

Many bridge players labor under the misconception that the best penalty doubles occur when you are loaded with

---

*If one of South's diamonds is exchanged for one of dummy's, the contract is cold regardless of the play at trick one. For example, suppose that the three and four of diamonds are switched. East tops the jack of clubs with the ace and returns the queen, but South simply wins with the king, plays the three of diamonds (now in dummy), and puts on the four from his hand. If the defenders don't ruff, South draws trumps and wins the rest of the tricks with good diamonds. If they do ruff, South still has a diamond left and can reach the dummy (and make his contract) after regaining the lead and drawing trumps.

trumps or high cards or both, and can expect to trounce the opponents without any help from your partner. For example, all of the following situations might seem to be ideal for a penalty double:

(a) Opponents bid 2 ♠
  ♠ K 10 5 3 2
  ♡ A K 9
  ◇ A 8 4
  ♣ 7 3

(b) Partner opens 1 ♠
    and RHO overcalls 2 ♡
  ♠ 6 5 2
  ♡ K Q 10 7 3 2
  ◇ 7 4
  ♣ Q 2

(c) Opponents bid 4 ♠
  ♠ A 9 2
  ♡ Q 9 2
  ◇ K Q 3 2
  ♣ A J 10

(d) Opponents bid 6 ♠
  ♠ A
  ♡ A 3 2
  ◇ A K J 10 9
  ♣ Q J 10 9

The odd truth, however, is that these cases are from actual play, and each contract was doubled *and made.* No doubt you'd like to see the full stories, so here they are.

PENALTY DOUBLES THAT BOOMERANGED

As my friend learned to his sorrow in the Prologue, it's a bad idea to alert an expert declarer to a trump stack. He opted to double 6 ♠ holding

    ♠ Q J 10 8
    ♡ K 10 3
    ◇ 9 8 2
    ♣ K 6 3

thinking that he had two "certain" trump tricks and a couple of

potential winners on the side. Declarer, alerted to the impend-
ing disaster by the double, studied the hand carefully and found
an unusual line of play that succeeded in overcoming the 4-0
trump split. As a result, the double cost my friend well over
1000 points—the difference between down one (the probable
result without the signal flare provided by the double) and
making the small slam. Here's a similar example, from a 1960
intercity match between New York and Los Angeles:

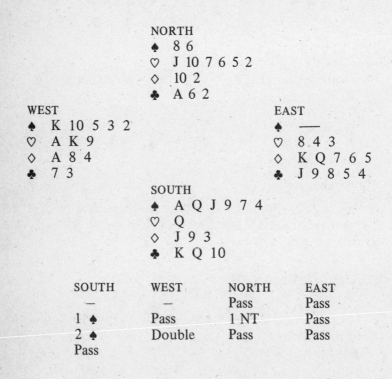

NORTH
♠ 8 6
♡ J 10 7 6 5 2
◇ 10 2
♣ A 6 2

WEST
♠ K 10 5 3 2
♡ A K 9
◇ A 8 4
♣ 7 3

EAST
♠ —
♡ 8 4 3
◇ K Q 7 6 5
♣ J 9 8 5 4

SOUTH
♠ A Q J 9 7 4
♡ Q
◇ J 9 3
♣ K Q 10

SOUTH	WEST	NORTH	EAST
—	—	Pass	Pass
1 ♠	Pass	1 NT	Pass
2 ♠	Double	Pass	Pass
Pass			

As we saw in Chapter 1, West's delayed double is for
penalties; it indicates that he was trap passing on the first round
of bidding with a good hand and substantial strength in the
enemy suit. Since Howard Schenken was in the South chair,
however, West should have left well enough alone! West led the

heart king and shifted to the seven of clubs, and South won in his hand and conceded a diamond trick. East captured it with his queen and, unable to lead a trump through declarer without borrowing one from another deck, tried another club. South won with dummy's ace, ruffed a heart, and conceded another diamond. East won with his king and led a club, West ruffed and played his ace of hearts, and South ruffed.

The defenders now had four tricks, and the position was:

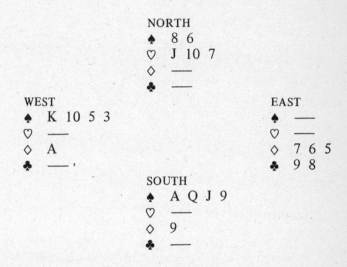

```
                      NORTH
                      ♠  8 6
                      ♡  J 10 7
                      ◇  —
                      ♣  —

WEST                                      EAST
♠  K 10 5 3                               ♠  —
♡  —                                      ♡  —
◇  A                                      ◇  7 6 5
♣  —                                      ♣  9 8

                      SOUTH
                      ♠  A Q J 9
                      ♡  —
                      ◇  9
                      ♣  —
```

South ruffed a diamond in dummy and played a spade to his jack, and the defenders were finished. If West won, he'd be endplayed; if he ducked, South would follow with the queen or nine of spades. Either way, West could get only one trick, and he needed two to defeat the contract.

Here's an even longer and stronger trump holding that produced the same dismal result—declarer was doubled into game and made it. The hand is from the 1970 playoff to determine the United States International Team, so you can be

sure that all the participants were taking matters *very* seriously.
South was Edgar Kaplan.

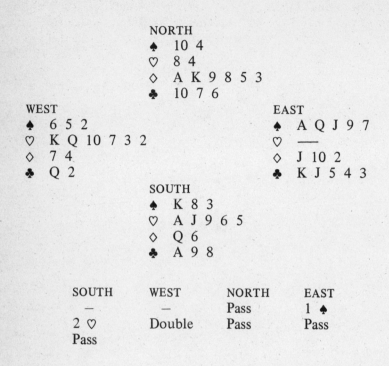

NORTH
♠ 10 4
♡ 8 4
♢ A K 9 8 5 3
♣ 10 7 6

WEST
♠ 6 5 2
♡ K Q 10 7 3 2
♢ 7 4
♣ Q 2

EAST
♠ A Q J 9 7
♡ —
♢ J 10 2
♣ K J 5 4 3

SOUTH
♠ K 8 3
♡ A J 9 6 5
♢ Q 6
♣ A 9 8

SOUTH	WEST	NORTH	EAST
—	—	Pass	1 ♠
2 ♡	Double	Pass	Pass
Pass			

South's hand is difficult to bid; the weak heart suit makes
an overcall dangerous, but passing with so much strength could
easily miss a laydown game. Things turned out quite well,
however, when West elected to lead a spade. (The opening lead
of the club queen defeats the contract, but no defender should
risk doubling the opponents into game when the outcome
depends on one unlikely play.) East won with the ace and
wanted very much to return a trump, but his cards wouldn't
cooperate. He actually played a low club; South ducked, won

the club return with his ace, played the king of spades and
ruffed a spade, and cashed the three high diamonds in order to
discard his losing club. West, reduced to his six trumps, had to
ruff the third diamond, and the position was.

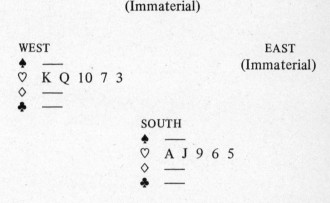

NORTH
(Immaterial)

WEST   EAST
♠ —   (Immaterial)
♡ K Q 10 7 3
◇ —
♣ —

SOUTH
♠ —
♡ A J 9 6 5
◇ —
♣ —

West needed three more tricks to defeat the contract, but
there was no way to get more than two. He led the heart king,
and South ducked. West followed with the heart three (as good
as anything at this point), and South won with the six and
returned the nine. West took his ten but was endplayed, and
had to concede the last two tricks—and the doubled contract.*

Even doubles of game with hands worth a strong notrump
opening bid can backfire badly. Here's an example from the

---

*It should be noted that East was also to blame for this disaster; he
should have anticipated the defenders' problems and pulled his partner's
double to 2 ♠.

final round of the New York 1972 Reisinger Knockout Team of
Four:

NORTH
♠ 8 6 3
♡ K 10
◇ 7
♣ K Q 6 5 4 3 2

WEST
♠ J 5
♡ J 8 7 4 3
◇ 10 6 4
♣ 9 8 7

EAST
♠ A 9 2
♡ Q 9 2
◇ K Q 3 2
♣ A J 10

SOUTH
♠ K Q 10 7 4
♡ A 6 5
◇ A J 9 8 5
♣ —

SOUTH	WEST	NORTH	EAST
1 ♠	Pass	2 ♣	Pass
2 ◇	Pass	2 ♠	Pass
3 ◇	Pass	3 ♠	Pass
4 ♠	Pass	Pass	Double
Redouble	Pass	Pass	Pass

East's double on scattered high-card strength was particularly unwise because his team was well ahead at the time this
hand arose. South, Sol Seidman of New York, seized the
opportunity to increase the possible reward (and the pressure)
by redoubling. West led a low heart, and South won with
dummy's king, played a diamond to the ace, and ruffed a
diamond, and led the king of clubs. East hopefully hopped up
with the ace, but South struck gloom into the enemies' hearts
by ruffing. He then cashed the heart ace, ruffed a diamond,
pitched a diamond on the queen of clubs, and ruffed a club
with the ten of spades. A heart was ruffed in dummy.

The position was:

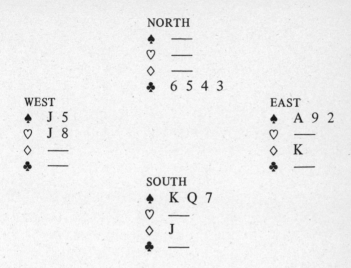

NORTH
♠ —
♡ —
◇ —
♣ 6 5 4 3

WEST
♠ J 5
♡ J 8
◇ —
♣ —

EAST
♠ A 9 2
♡ —
◇ K
♣ —

SOUTH
♠ K Q 7
♡ —
◇ J
♣ —

A club was led from dummy, and East was helpless. Ruffing with the ace of trumps wouldn't help, so he discarded his diamond. South ruffed with the spade queen, shutting out West's jack, and exited with a diamond. East ruffed and cashed his ace of trumps, but had to concede the last trick to South's king of spades. Making the redoubled contract with an overtrick was worth a sensational 1030 points; and the bonanza on this deal turned out to be just enough to give Seidman's team, captained by David Mason of New Jersey, a startling come-from-behind victory in New York's most prestigious tournament event.*

Finally, here's a hand from a Virginia tournament that undoubtedly left East talking to himself for weeks.

*A trump lead and return will stop the overtrick, but not the contract (or the ultimate victory by the Mason team). South ruffs one diamond in dummy, plays the king of clubs and ruffs out East's ace, draws the last trump, gives up two diamond tricks, and eventually discards his losing heart on the queen of clubs. East *would* have won the championship, however, by declining to double 4 ♠.

NORTH
- ♠ Q J 10 2
- ♡ K Q J 10 9 7 5
- ◇ —
- ♣ A 4

WEST
- ♠ 7 4
- ♡ 8 6 4
- ◇ Q 8 5 4
- ♣ 7 6 3 2

EAST
- ♠ A
- ♡ A 3 2
- ◇ A K J 10 9
- ♣ Q J 10 9

SOUTH
- ♠ K 9 8 6 5 3
- ♡ —
- ◇ 7 6 3 2
- ♣ K 8 5

SOUTH	WEST	NORTH	EAST
—	—	—	1 ◇
1 ♠	Pass	3 ♡	Pass
3 ♠	Pass	6 ♠	Double
Pass	Pass	Pass	

North, Frank Mastrola of Baltimore, forced in hearts after his partner's spade overcall, then jumped directly to slam. East doubled, licking his chops, but it was his wounds that were soon in need of attention!

PENALTIES FROM NOWHERE

The frequency with which apparently superb penalty doubles backfire may seem astonishing. The other side of the coin, however, can be equally surprising, for there are times when doubles on meager trump holdings (such as J 4 2 or even 9 7 5) or just a modicum of high-card strength can produce devastating penalties! For example (both sides vulnerable):

NORTH
♠ 6 4 3
♡ Q 7 6 2
♢ 6 3
♣ 8 7 4 3

WEST
♠ 9 2
♡ A 9 8
♢ J 4 2
♣ A J 9 6 2

EAST
♠ A K 8 7 5
♡ K J 10
♢ Q 7 5
♣ 10 5

SOUTH
♠ Q J 10
♡ 5 4 3
♢ A K 10 9 8
♣ K Q

SOUTH	WEST	NORTH	EAST
—	—	—	1 ♠
2 ♢	Double	Pass	Pass
Pass			

West didn't know quite what to do over South's 2 ♢ overcall: 3 ♣ would be an overbid, his spade support was too poor for a raise, and he couldn't bid notrump with no diamond stoppers. After some thought, he decided to double—and wound up with a 1100-point jackpot! He led a spade, and East cashed his two winners and gave West a spade ruff. West then laid down the ace of clubs, followed with the ace of hearts, and played another heart. East took two more heart tricks and cleverly returned a spade, and South had to lose two trump tricks.*

*Playing negative doubles, West passes, East protects his partner by reopening with a double, and West passes for penalties. The club weakness makes East's reopening double somewhat risky, but he knows West will bend over backwards to bid a major suit if he pulls the double.

Here's another example (both sides vulnerable):

```
                        NORTH
                        ♠ K J 6 4 2
                        ♡ A K J
                        ◇ J 4
                        ♣ 8 5 2
        WEST                                    EAST
        ♠ 5 3                                   ♠ A Q 10 9
        ♡ 10 9 8 4                              ♡ 7 6 2
        ◇ K 9 8 7 6                             ◇ 5
        ♣ K 6                                   ♣ Q J 10 9 3
                        SOUTH
                        ♠ 8 7
                        ♡ Q 5 3
                        ◇ A Q 10 3 2
                        ♣ A 7 4
```

SOUTH	WEST	NORTH	EAST
—	—	1 ♠	Pass
2 ◇	Pass	2 ♠	Pass
2 NT	Pass	3 NT	Double
Pass	Pass	Pass	

East kept a keen ear tuned to the bidding, and drew some very profitable conclusions. The opponents seemed to be straining to reach game and were unlikely to have much in reserve; his spades were ideally located behind North's strength; whatever diamond strength his side might own was well placed in West's hand, so South would lose any finesses in that suit; and he had a fine-looking club suit that might produce some tricks. West, alerted by the double to the fact that East owned strength in dummy's bid suit, properly led a spade instead of attacking from his feeble heart suit. The defenders wound up with three spade tricks, four club tricks, and the king of diamonds—and 1100 points.

For our final example, let's suppose that the auction proceeds as follows:

YOU	LHO	PARTNER	RHO
—	—	—	1 ♡
Pass	Pass	Double	Pass
Pass	2 ♣	Double	2 ◇
?			

The opponents are vulnerable, and you hold

```
♠  K 5 4
♡  A Q J 9 8
◇  9 7 5
♣  10 9
```

Passing 1 ♡ doubled for penalties wasn't hard, but what now? You seem to have the opponents on the run, as partner's penalty double of 2 ♣ was pulled by a frightened RHO, but your diamonds appear to be much too weak for a double of 2 ◇. However, there are several indications that a juicy penalty is in the offing. Partner's balancing double promises a few cards in diamonds; the deal appears to be a misfit; LHO's initial pass indicates extreme weakness; and declarer will have a difficult time ruffing hearts in dummy because partner is likely to overruff. As it happens, the double nets 800 points, for the complete deal is:

NORTH
♠ 10 3 2
♡ 7
◇ J 4 2
♣ Q 6 5 4 3 2

WEST
♠ K 5 4
♡ A Q J 9 8
◇ 9 7 5
♣ 10 9

EAST
♠ Q J 7 6
♡ 6 4
◇ Q 10 6
♣ A K J 8

SOUTH
♠ A 9 8
♡ K 10 5 3 2
◇ A K 8 3
♣ 7

SOUTH	WEST	NORTH	EAST
1 ♡	Pass	Pass	Double
Pass	Pass	2 ♣	Double
2 ◇	Double	Pass	Pass
Pass			

West led the ten of clubs, which held the trick, and followed with the club nine. South ruffed and led a low heart in a desperate attempt to secure some ruffs in dummy (and some tricks). West won with the eight and returned a low spade. South topped East's jack with the ace, ruffed a heart, played a diamond to the ace, and ruffed another heart with the jack of diamonds. East, however, overruffed with the queen and returned a spade to West's king. West fired back another spade, and East took his queen and played the ace of clubs. South ruffed with the eight, but West overruffed with the nine and threw South back in his hand with a trump in order to collect the last two tricks in hearts. Down three!

Doubling Strategy

What went wrong in the examples where solid-looking penalty doubles boomeranged? And what went right in the cases where apparently shaky doubles reaped rich dividends? Let's examine some of the key factors that determine whether or not a penalty double is likely to be a good risk.

THE ABILITY OF THE OPPONENTS

If your opponents are good players, holding some extra high cards or trumps by no means indicates that a lucrative penalty is in the offing. For one thing, competent opponents should be reasonably on target during the bidding, so they may well have unexpected compensating values that will render your high cards useless (such as a void in a key side suit at a trump contract, or a long and solid suit that will take a depressingly large number of tricks). Also, if they do happen to have blundered into an absurd contract, your double may give them a chance to escape to a makeable one. Finally, as we have seen, good declarers can bring home very unlikely looking contracts when warned about the existing distribution by a penalty double.

Against weaker opponents, however, you need not be so cautious. Declarer is unlikely to pull any endplays, coups, or rabbits out of his hat; in fact, he may even drop an extra trick or two because he is flustered by the double (and/or an abysmal trump split). In addition, such opponents may have arrived at a contract so poor that there is no way to avoid a substantial penalty even with all four hands exposed.

YOUR SIDE'S DEFENSIVE ABILITY

Golf hustlers know that the typical weekend player is more likely to miss a short putt when the pressure is increased by a sizeable bet. Similarly, many bridge players defend more poorly under the increased stress created by their own penalty double, particularly if they have doubled a part-score contract that will produce game if it is fulfilled. Defense is the hardest part of bridge; if you have trouble with it, *don't* light the fuse of your own petard by making close penalty doubles.

HOW YOUR SIDE'S STRENGTH IS DIVIDED

Having all the strength concentrated in one hand is likely to be bad for the defense. The doubler's partner will never be able to lead through any enemy soft spots, and declarer can tell in advance which finesses will win and which will lose by simply playing the doubler for any missing high cards. If, however, the doubler's partner has some strength, he can cooperate effectively in the defense, and declarer may run into some very unpleasant surprises.

HOW THE OPPONENTS' STRENGTH IS DIVIDED

Similarly, the opponents are more likely to be in trouble if the bidding shows that most of their strength is concentrated in one hand. If declarer lacks any entries to dummy, he will have to conduct his campaign by leading away from his own tenaces—an embarrassing fate that is likely to prove extremely profitable for the defenders. If, however, the enemy strength is fairly evenly divided, declarer is likely to have the luxury of ample entries to both hands, and he may well be able to bring home his contract by taking some highly effective finesses.

THE LOCATION OF YOUR SIDE'S
HIGH CARDS

If South has bid clubs, for example, and you are West and hold ♣ A Q 10 8, things are in great shape. Even if the enemy winds up in a different denomination, you will be able to capture South's high clubs because you play after him, so you may well wind up with three or four tricks in the suit. If, however, you are in the East chair, your prospects are much more bleak, for declarer will surely lead the suit from dummy and force you to play before he does. Thus, it is clearly better for the defensive strength to be located *behind* the opponent who is also marked with strength.

HOW YOUR SIDE'S TRUMPS ARE DIVIDED

Similarly, it is better for the defender who is sitting behind the opponent with long trumps to also be long and strong in trumps, so that he can win finesses and score overruffs. Having all of the defenders' trumps in one hand, however, is likely to be a *dis*advantage, for the doubler's partner will not be able to make even one valuable trump lead through the enemy strength. Thus, it may seem better for the defense if West holds K Q 10 7 3 2 in trumps and East is void, but superior results are likely to be obtained—at least against good players—if West has K Q 10 7 and East has 3 2.

THE SIZE OF YOUR LOW TRUMP SPOTS

Watch the size of your low trump spots, especially against low-level contracts. For example, a trump holding like K 10 9 8 7 is much better than K 10 5 3 2, and K Q 10 9 8 3 is significantly better than K Q 10 7 3 2. The reasons for this are that solidity in the trump suit makes a fatal endplay by declarer less likely; it makes overruffs of declarer more likely; and it allows you to lead trumps yourself in the event that it is necessary to eliminate ruffing power in dummy.

YOUR DEFENSIVE STRENGTH AGAINST
OTHER CONTRACTS

It's usually a poor idea to double an overcall for penalties unless you have defensive strength against more than one contract. For example, if your partner opens with 1 ♠ and your right-hand opponent overcalls with 2 ♡, pass holding

♠ 6 2
♡ Q J 10 8 6 3
◊ 6 5 2
♣ 9 7

You can probably defeat 2 ♡, but someone is likely to be void in hearts and hurriedly run out to a different suit. If the escape artist turns out to be your left-hand opponent, partner will be highly displeased if he doubles the new contract only to see the opponents wrap it up because you have no defensive tricks at all! However, with

♠ 6 2
♡ A J 9 7
◊ A 10 6 3
♣ 9 4 2

by all means make a penalty double of 2 ♡ (or pass and then pass partner's reopening double for penalties if you are using negative doubles). Your aces will be fine defensive values against any contract, so you will be more than happy to hear partner double an escape bid by the opponents—and partner should be delighted with the result.

IS THE DEAL A MISFIT?

Misfits spell trouble for whichever side declares the contract, for terrible suit splits and unexpected ruffs and overruffs are likely to abound. Thus, if you can visualize that the opponents are in serious trouble (as was the case in the last of the example hands), even weak trumps may be sufficient for a crushing penalty double. However, watch out for an auction like

YOU	LHO	PARTNER	RHO
—	—	1 ♠	2 ♣
Double	Pass	Pass	2 ◇
Double	Pass	Pass	2 ♡
?			

Assuming that you have made penalty doubles with strength in clubs and diamonds, you should pass if you are weak in hearts. Some wise guys like to fool around with auctions like this one when holding a solid eight-card heart suit in the hope that you'll fall into the trap of doubling 2 ♡ out of habit. Partner has heard the auction, and he'll double if he has strong hearts.

ARE YOU DOUBLING THE OPPONENTS INTO GAME?

A penalty double of an enemy 2 ♣ or 2 ◇ contract can be more speculative than a double of a part-score bid of 2 ♡ or higher, because the opponents will not score a game even if the contract is made. However, don't become a bridge agent 007 by issuing yourself a license to double 2 ♣ or 2 ◇ in any and all situations; doubled overtricks can be very expensive, and the opponents will in fact register a game if they redouble and make their contract.

YOUR LENGTH IN PARTNER'S BID SUIT

Shortness in the suit bid by your partner is a great asset for making a penalty double of a suit contract. It reduces the chances that the opponents will be able to ruff away the high cards that partner is likely to have in his bid suit, and it may also enable you to score some tricks with your low trumps by ruffing.

On the other side of the coin, length in partner's suit should warn you away from a low-level penalty double of a suit contract. My friend went astray in the Prologue when his partner opened with 1 ♠, his right-hand opponent overcalled 2 ◇, and he doubled holding

♠ J 10 7 4
♡ J 9 8
♢ A K 3 2
♣ 10 9

His spade length ruined his partner's A K Q, for declarer was predictably short and ruffed in on the second round of the suit, and he never did get to score any useful ruffs with his low trumps. His correct action, therefore, was to raise his partner's opening bid. The moral: *Bid the limit in your own suit before doubling the opponents unless you see a sure profit.*

DO YOU HAVE A NASTY SURPRISE FOR THE OPPONENTS?

Holding the A K of trumps may give you a nice, warm feeling, but douse yourself in ice water before you double an enemy overcall. Your opponent knew perfectly well that he was missing these cards when he chose to bid, so he should have good compensation (such as a suit like Q J 10 9 3 2, or a strong two-suited hand). Given a choice, it is better to double holding Q J 10 9 of trumps than A K 3 2. The loss of two trump tricks is much more likely to come as a nasty (and fatal) shock to declarer in the former instance, and your two sure defensive tricks use up only three of your side's high-card points.

DO THE OPPONENTS HAVE A NASTY SURPRISE FOR YOU?

If the opponents stagger into game after an unimpressive auction, they probably don't have much more than the 26 points needed to bid game (and they may even be a little short). For example, an auction like

YOU	LHO	PARTNER	RHO
—	—	—	1 ♡
Pass	1 ♠	Pass	2 ♣
Pass	2 ♡	Pass	2 NT
Pass	3 ♡	Pass	4 ♡
?			

suggests that the opponents don't have much to spare, and a double may well strike oil if you're well off in hearts and clubs. If, however, the opponents zip into game after an auction such as 1 ♠/3 ♠/4 ♠, they may well have extra values, so don't make a penalty double unless you have a very good reason.

THE VULNERABILITY

Experienced bridge players always keep a close eye on the vulnerability. We saw in Chapter 1 that you can be somewhat more aggressive if you are not vulnerable, but should be more conservative if you are vulnerable. Similarly, a penalty double has more to gain if the opponents are vulnerable; whereas if you are vulnerable and the opponents are not, it may well be best for you to go after your own game contract.

A Concluding Note

Keeping these guidelines in mind should help you avoid disastrous penalty doubles, and find some unexpected bonanzas by detecting when the enemy is in trouble. If you are in doubt, *don't* double; it's easier to tolerate a 300-point penalty that should have been 800 than it is to explain to an angry partner why your double of 2 ♡ let the opponents chalk up a game for taking just eight tricks. Make a mental note of situations in which you thought a double might work out well, and keep track of the results. If you find that there are certain instances

in which you pass but consistently score three-trick or
four-trick sets, you can safely expand your coverage by
doubling when such a case comes up again.

Doubles of Overcalls: Unilateral Commands vs. Flexible Proposals to Partner

Some penalty doubles of enemy overcalls virtually command partner to pass. Others are more flexible, and permit him
to overrule your decision if he has a good reason (such as a void
in trumps, meager defensive values, and a good escape suit).

UNILATERAL PENALTY DOUBLES

Your double of an overcall by the opponents conveys a
strict order to pass in any of the following situations:

1. *Partner has made a preemptive bid.* After making a
preemptive bid, partner is expected to retire from the auction
and turn full control over to you; if you double an enemy
overcall, he must pass. Since his bid shows little or no defensive
strength, you'd better be able to defeat the opponents in your
own hand if you want to maintain partnership harmony (and
win the rubber). For example (neither side vulnerable):

YOU	LHO	PARTNER	RHO
—	—	4 ♣	4 ♡
?			

(a) ♠ 7 6 3   (b) ♠ A J 3
    ♡ K Q 10   ♡ Q J 9 7
    ◇ A 9 4 3   ◇ A K 8 4 3
    ♣ 7 6 2   ♣ 4

You should pass with hand (a). Remember that partner's
4 ♣ opening bid shows a hand like

♠ 10 4 2
♡ —
♢ 7 6
♣ K Q J 10 9 8 5 3

The most you are likely to get is a one-trick set, so a
double has little to gain. And for all you know, your left-hand
opponent may be about to fall victim to the confusion created
by your partner's preempt and make a disastrous try for slam.

In example (b), however, your right-hand opponent has
clearly guessed wrong under the pressure created by your
partner's preempt. Cash in on his blunder by making a penalty
double.

2. *Partner has made a strong two-bid.* If partner happily
opens the bidding with a strong two-bid (or an artificial 2 ♣ bid
if you prefer that procedure) and the next player is fearless (or
foolhardy) enough to overcall, a double insists that partner pass
unless he has freakish distribution and can make game in his
own hand. For example (you are vulnerable):

YOU	LHO	PARTNER	RHO
—	—	2 ♣	2 ♠
?			

Regardless of whether partner's strong 2 ♣ bid is natural
or artificial, you should double with either of the following
hands:

(a) ♠ Q J 10 7   (b) ♠ Q J 8 6 5 3
    ♡ 9 7 6 4 3   ♡ 7 3
    ♢ 9 8   ♢ 6 2
    ♣ 4 3   ♣ 5 4 3

Unlike the double of an overcall of a one-level opening bid, which promises some defense against any contract that the opponents may stumble into, this double informs partner that your hand can be filed in the waste basket unless your side defends against 2 ♠. Thus, you must be careful *not* to double with a hand like

(c) ♠ Q J 6 3
     ♡ A K 4
     ◇ 4 3
     ♣ J 9 7 2

Here, your high-card strength will be quite useful in a contract of your own, and the vulnerability argues against playing for penalties. Partner would pass a double with a hand like

     ♠ —
     ♡ 8 5 2
     ◇ A K Q J
     ♣ A K Q 10 8 6

because he could not guarantee making a game opposite a near Yarborough; and while you would probably collect around 700 points by defending against 2 ♠ doubled, you can rack up three times as much by bidding your laydown grand slam in clubs. With hand (c), therefore, your best bet is to pass; partner can't conceivably let the bidding die with his powerhouse, and you'll be in a better position to decide what to do after he describes his hand further.

3. *You repeat a penalty double after partner has pulled it.* If you make a penalty double that partner is permitted to pull and he does so, and the opponents obstinately persist by bidding more of their suit, a repeated double by you commands partner to pass and ensures that you can defeat the enemy contract in your own hand. Since partner wouldn't have run from your first double unless his hand was very unsuitable for defense, you must be absolutely certain that the opponents are headed down the drain before you double for the second time.

4. *Partner has opened with a notrump bid.* An opening bid

of 1 NT describes partner's hand very precisely, so you are in full charge of the subsequent auction. The most important requirement to double an overcall of partner's 1 NT bid is *good trumps*; and, assuming that partner's bid is of the standard 15-17 or 16-18 point variety, an additional side high card or two should be sufficient. For example (both sides vulnerable):

YOU	LHO	PARTNER	RHO
—	—	1 NT	2 ♠
?			

(a) ♠ 7 4   (b) ♠ Q 10 8 6
    ♡ K 8 6 2   ♡ 5 2
    ♢ 5 4 3 2   ♢ A 10 8
    ♣ K J 2   ♣ J 10 9 4

In example (a), you have little choice but to pass. It might be your hand, but there isn't much you can do about it. A double could easily be catastrophic because of your poor spades, for most opponents don't enter the auction after a 1 NT opening bid unless they have a strong suit and a great many playing tricks, and there is no good constructive bid that you can make.

With hand (b), however, you should double. Partner must have a couple of spades in addition to his substantial strength, since his 1 NT opening bid denies any voids or singletons, so your right-hand opponent should soon be *very* sorry that he opened his mouth at all!

Overcalls of a 2 NT opening bid are few and far between. If you ever run into one, double to show a hand with strength primarily located in the enemy suit.

5. *You have doubled an insufficient bid.* This actually happened at a recent tournament: North opened the bidding with 3 ♠ ; East, who had perhaps indulged a bit too freely during dinner, undercalled with 3 ♡ (!). South held:

    ♠ 6
    ♡ A Q 7 2
    ♢ J 9 6 3
    ♣ A K Q 2

Even in a World Championship, East would be permitted to correct his bid to 4 ♡ if he did so in the same breath, so South properly waited for a few moments to see if East was aware of his gaffe. When silence prevailed, however, South had a golden opportunity—but he blew it by calling for the tournament director! That official properly ruled that there would be no penalty if East corrected his bid to 4 ♡; but if he did anything else, West would be barred from the bidding for the remainder of the auction. South, of course, was hoping to get a crack at 4 ♡; but East took a skeptical look at his unimpressive hand and elected to change his bid to a pass in spite of the muzzling effect that this would have on his partner. As a result, South lost his chance at a lucrative penalty.

South failed to realize that once he had paused briefly to give East a chance to correct his mistake, it was perfectly legal and ethical to double 3 ♡ for penalties. This would prohibit East from changing his bid even if he subsequently became aware of his error. And the ensuing penalty would have won a top score for North and South.

FLEXIBLE PENALTY DOUBLES

Most other penalty doubles are *not* unilateral commands, and partner may overrule you if he has a good reason. (The question of when to pull a penalty double and when to sit for it will be discussed in the next chapter.) These include:

Doubles of suit overcalls. The strategy of doubling suit overcalls by the opponents has been discussed previously. But a few additional points are worth noting:

The higher the level at which you double for penalties, the less partner is expected to cooperate in the decision. Thus, it is reasonable to make a speculative double of a 2 ◇ overcall, for partner will surely pull it with a minimum opening bid and a void in diamonds. But you should clearly foresee a set in order to double a 4 ♡ preempt, for partner usually cannot afford to start shopping around for a fit at the four-level or five-level.

It's a good idea *not* to let an overcall talk you out of an action that would have been obvious had your opponent maintained a discreet silence. For example, if partner opens with 1 ♣ and your right-hand opponent overcalls with 1 ◇, make your normal 1 ♡ bid with

♠ Q 3
♡ A 10 6 2
◇ K J 9 3
♣ 4 3 2

Doubles of 1 NT overcalls. A 1 NT overcall shows an impressive hand—one worth an opening bid of 1 NT. All is not lost, however, for partner's opening bid represents a plus for your side. Since he should have at least 13 points and your right-hand opponent promises at least 16 points, the most you can expect to have in high cards is about 11 points. If you do have this many, RHO should be in terrible trouble, for his dummy will be barren and he'll have to keep leading from his hand (and away from his tenaces). Thus, if partner opens the bidding with 1 ♠ and your right-hand opponent overcalls with 1 NT, you should be delighted to double with either of the following hands:

(a) ♠ Q 6 2   (b) ♠ 10 9
     ♡ A 8 4 3   ♡ A Q 10 6 2
     ◇ K 10 6   ◇ 6 4
     ♣ Q 9 8   ♣ K 10 8 3

To double, you need about 8 high-card points; and length and strength in partner's suit *is* desirable, since no one can ruff anything in a notrump contract.

Note that after the above auction, you can safely compete by bidding 2 ♡ with a hand like

♠ J 7
♡ Q J 10 8 6 2
◇ 6 4 3
♣ 5 2

Your failure to double warns partner that you have a weak hand of less than 8 points.

Doubles of cue-bids. Doubles of direct cue-bids by an opponent after partner opens with one of a suit don't occur often enough to warrant extensive discussion. Generally, such doubles show a strong interest in doubling whatever contract the opponents finally arrive at. For example, if partner opens with 1 ♡ and your right-hand opponent makes a Michaels Cue-Bid of 2 ♡, showing 5-5 or better distribution with the length in spades and an unspecified minor suit, double with

> ♠ K J 10 6
> ♡ 7 2
> ◇ Q J 10 9
> ♣ K Q 3

You would very much like the opportunity to double the opponents for penalties regardless of whether they wind up in spades or in a minor suit, and your double of 2 ♡ warns partner against interfering with your plans.

Doubles of 1 NT Opening Bids

A double of an enemy 1 NT opening bid is for penalties, and promises at least as much strength as that shown by your opponent. It is also desirable to have a *good opening lead,* such as a solid sequence; 1 NT contracts are the hardest of all to defend against, and you'll very much appreciate being able to get off to a good start. For example, suppose your right-hand opponent opens with 1 NT, showing 16-18 points, and you hold any of the following hands:

(a)		(b)		(c)	
♠	9 8	♠	K 9 8	♠	K 10 3
♡	K Q J 10 3	♡	A Q 2	♡	A 9 2
◇	A K Q	◇	K J 7 3	◇	Q J 8 6
♣	K 10 3	♣	K J 2	♣	K J 2

A double is ideal with hand (a); you have impressive values and no trouble planning the defense. Some experts would also double with hand (b), but a pass is likely to be the winning action; you have no good opening lead, and you're likely to wind up making several ruinous leads into declarer's tenaces. With hand (c), a pass is clear-cut.

On occasion, this double has been used to set a trap for the unwary:

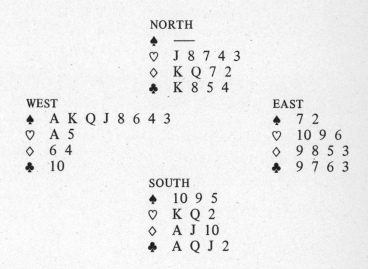

NORTH
♠ —
♡ J 8 7 4 3
◇ K Q 7 2
♣ K 8 5 4

WEST
♠ A K Q J 8 6 4 3
♡ A 5
◇ 6 4
♣ 10

EAST
♠ 7 2
♡ 10 9 6
◇ 9 8 5 3
♣ 9 7 6 3

SOUTH
♠ 10 9 5
♡ K Q 2
◇ A J 10
♣ A Q J 2

When this deal was played in a New York bridge club, South dealt and opened the bidding with 1 NT. As a result, West wasn't too hopeful about finding his partner with the one additional trick he needed for game, so he baited his noose by doubling. North, who had been taught to redouble in this situation with 7 or more high-card points, failed to recognize the significance of his spade void and saw no reason to deviate from standard operating procedures. East, regretting the day he ever learned to play bridge, had little choice but to pass, and South saw no reason to take any action.

Down three—redoubled! And with North-South cold for *slam!*

Review Quiz

In each of the following problems, the vulnerability and bidding are shown. What call do you make?

(1)   Both sides vulnerable

YOU	LHO	PARTNER	RHO	You hold:
—	—	1 ♡	2 ◊	♠ 10 9 3
?				♡ 6
				◊ K J 9 5
				♣ A 6 4 3 2

(2)   You are vulnerable

YOU	LHO	PARTNER	RHO	You hold:
—	—	1 ♡	2 ◊	♠ K Q 8
?				♡ 7 4 3
				◊ K Q 4
				♣ A J 5 2

(3)   Neither side vulnerable

YOU	LHO	PARTNER	RHO	You hold:
—	—	1 ♡	2 ◊	♠ 6 4
?				♡ K 10 6 2
				◊ K J 9 5
				♣ 8 5 3

(4)   Neither side vulnerable

YOU	LHO	PARTNER	RHO	You hold:
—	—	1 ♠	2 ♣	♠ 6
?				♡ A 4 2
				◇ A 8 6 5 3 2
				♣ J 10 7

(5)   Opponents are vulnerable

YOU	LHO	PARTNER	RHO	You hold:
—	—	1 ♠	2 ♣	♠ 8 5 4
?				♡ 7 2
				◇ 6 3
				♣ K J 8 7 4 3

(6)   Neither side vulnerable

YOU	LHO	PARTNER	RHO	You hold:
—	1 NT	Pass	3 NT	♠ A 9 8
?				♡ K J 7
				◇ A 6 4 3
				♣ Q 5 4

(7)   Opponents are vulnerable

YOU	LHO	PARTNER	RHO	You hold:
—	—	1 ♠	4 ♡	♠ 8 2
?				♡ A J 10 8
				◇ Q 6 5 2
				♣ 10 9 5

(8) Both sides vulnerable

YOU	LHO	PARTNER	RHO	You hold:
1 ♠	2 ◇	Double*	Pass	♠ A K 6 4 3
Pass	2 ♡	Double*	3 ♣	♡ A 5 3
?				◇ Q 2
		*Penalties		♣ J 9 7

(9) Both sides vulnerable

YOU	LHO	PARTNER	RHO	You hold:
—	—	—	1 ♠	♠ Q J 10 9
Pass	2 ♣	Pass	2 ◇	♡ 10 9 8
Pass	2 ♠	Pass	3 ♠	◇ A Q 10 6
Pass	4 ♠	Pass	Pass	♣ 3 2
?				

(10) Both sides vulnerable

YOU	LHO	PARTNER	RHO	You hold:
—	—	—	1 ♡	♠ 6 3 2
Pass	3 ♡	Pass	4 ◇	♡ K J 10 2
Pass	4 ♡	Pass	Pass	◇ 8 5 2
?				♣ K Q 6

(11) You are vulnerable

YOU	LHO	PARTNER	RHO	You hold:
—	—	2 ♣	2 ♡	♠ Q 3
?				♡ K 10 8 2
				◇ A 9 6 4
				♣ J 10 5

(12) Neither side vulnerable

YOU	LHO	PARTNER	RHO
—	—	—	1 NT
?			

You hold:
- ♠ A K
- ♡ A 10 7
- ◊ K Q J 9 7
- ♣ Q 8 3

(13) Opponents are vulnerable

YOU	LHO	PARTNER	RHO
—	—	3 ♠	4 ♡
?			

You hold:
- ♠ 6 4
- ♡ A Q 3
- ◊ K Q 8 2
- ♣ 7 6 4 3

(14) Opponents are vulnerable

YOU	LHO	PARTNER	RHO
—	—	3 ♠	4 ♡
?			

You hold:
- ♠ 7 2
- ♡ K J 10 7
- ◊ A K
- ♣ A 7 6 4 3

(15) Both sides vulnerable

YOU	LHO	PARTNER	RHO
—	Pass	Pass	1 ♡
Pass	2 ♣	Pass	2 ♡
Pass	2 NT	Pass	3 NT
?			

You hold:
- ♠ 10 4 2
- ♡ A Q 10 8
- ◊ Q J 10 9 8
- ♣ 5

Solutions

1. *Double using standard methods; pass if using negative doubles.* This is an ideal time to try for a penalty. You have fine trumps, shortness in partner's suit, and a side ace. If you are using negative doubles, pass and wait for partner to reopen with a double, which you will pass.

2. *Three notrump.* In view of the vulnerability, you would have to defeat 2 ◊ doubled *four* tricks to top the value of your own game. Unless RHO is notorious for his lunatic overcalls, 3 NT should bring in the most points.

3. *Two hearts.* Tend to avoid penalty doubles until you have bid the limit in your own suit. Your diamonds are impressive, but your length in partner's suit is terrible for defense against a suit contract.

4. *Double using standard methods; pass if using negative doubles.* An additional club would be nice, but there's a good chance for a respectable penalty as things stand in view if your two aces and singleton in partner's suit.

5. *Pass.* Don't double an overcall of partner's opening bid of one of a suit with defense against only one denomination. Someone is bound to pull a double of 2 ♣; and if it is LHO, partner is likely to make a catastrophic double of the escape bid because he expects some defensive strength from you.

6. *Pass.* Having all the strength concentrated in one hand is bad for the defense, as you're likely to be subjected to some devastating endplays and squeezes—especially if you tip your hand by doubling. Partner is almost sure to be broke, and you have no reason to think you can win five tricks.

7. *Double.* Doubles of high-level enemy preemptive overcalls do *not* invite partner's cooperation, so it should be safe to try and increase the penalty.

8. *Double.* The opponents are in terrible trouble, so don't let them off the hook. Partner has the red suits locked up, and you have three solid defensive tricks. If RHO had really good clubs, he probably would have bid them directly over the double of 2 ◊.

9. *Double.* You have a nasty surprise for declarer in trumps, your diamonds appear to be well located behind his strength, and any high cards your side may have in clubs are well positioned behind the club bidder.

10. *Pass.* Your right-hand opponent's bid of 4 ◊ was a slam try, so he should have ample strength in reserve. As it happens, *five* hearts can be made on an endplay, for the opponents' hands are:

LHO	RHO
♠ A Q 8	♠ K 7
♡ 9 7 4 3	♡ A Q 8 6 5
◊ K 9 6	◊ A J 7 4 3
♣ A 8 2	♣ 7

11. *Pass.* Going after your own game or slam should be your most profitable course in view of the vulnerability, and a double would order partner to pass. Since partner has made a strong two-bid, he can't let the auction die until at least game (or a satisfactory double of an enemy contract) is reached.

12. *Double.* You have a fine hand and an excellent opening lead, the king of diamonds.

13. *Pass.* Partner is likely to have no defensive tricks at all.

14. *Double.* If partner pulls it, shop around for a new partner! After he has preempted, the double of an overcall is an absolute command to pass.

15. *Double.* Success is not guaranteed, but all the signs are right. The opponents have staggered into game and should have little strength in reserve (RHO has a minimum, and LHO couldn't even open the bidding), the hearts and clubs appear to be breaking very badly for declarer, and your diamond suit is highly promising. Your double shows strength in RHO's bid suit, so partner should lead hearts rather than attacking from a nondescript spade suit. You will win the first trick and start setting up the diamonds.

5

Competitive Judgement

♠ ♡ ◇ ♣

Another unusual fact about penalty doubles is that some of the best ones are foiled not by the opponents, as you might expect, but by the doubler's own partner. Sometimes, he snatches defeat from the jaws of victory by pulling a double that was about to bring in a huge number of points; on other occasions, he fiendishly inserts a bid for no particularly good reason which prevents his partner, (who is looking at three or four tricks in the enemy suit), from making the killing penalty double in the first place. The best way to avoid sad fates like these, preserve harmony in your partnership, and rack up profits on your side of the score sheet, is to know when you should take charge of the auction yourself and when it is preferable to leave the decision to your partner.

Competitive Decisions: Bidding, Doubling, and the Forcing Pass

FORCING AUCTIONS

Suppose that only your side is vulnerable, and the auction proceeds:

YOU	LHO	PARTNER	RHO
1 ♠	4 ♡	4 ♠	5 ♡
?			

A little thought should convince you that it cannot be right for your side to sell out to 5 ♡ undoubled. Examine the evidence: Your side has bid a vulnerable game, and should therefore have a decided superiority in strength. Why, then, are your opponents bidding at the five-level? Apparently, they are so convinced that you will make 4 ♠ that they would rather sacrifice a small amount of points by going down, not vulnerable, in 5 ♡. Therefore, if you elect to pass and your left-hand opponent also passes, partner is obligated to take some action; he must either go on to 5 ♠ or, at the very least, increase the prospective penalty by doubling 5 ♡. Thus, your pass is *forcing,* and situations like this one are therefore called *forcing auctions.*

Here's another example (you are vulnerable):

YOU	LHO	PARTNER	RHO
1 ♠	Pass	3 ♠	5 ♡
?			

This time, your right-hand opponent is so pessimistic about his defensive prospects that he is not even waiting for you to get to 4 ♠ before he sacrifices. He hopes that by acting immediately, and thereby depriving your side of the opportunity to exchange additional information at the four-level, he will create enough confusion and chaos to permanently derail your bidding. One good way to strike back is to recognize that the auction is forcing, so you can pass and let partner figure out what to do if you are in doubt.

The concept of a forcing auction should not come as a bolt from the blue, for we encountered an example in Chapter 4:

YOU	LHO	PARTNER	RHO
—	—	2 ♣	2 ♠
?			

Partner's strong two-bid obligates your partnership to continue bidding until game, or a doubled enemy contract, has been reached. Therefore, the auction (and a pass by you) is forcing.

In a forcing auction, you have three methods at your disposal for overcoming the interference by the enemy: You can take charge by bidding, take charge by doubling, or use the invaluable forcing pass to let your partner make the decision. We will consider each in turn.

TAKING CHARGE BY BIDDING

On occasion, your hand will be so much more valuable on offense than on defense that you should take control of the auction by bidding. Some clues that will alert you to the need for this unilateral action include:

1. *A proven fit.* Floundering around at the five-level or six-level looking for a good suit to play in is likely to enrich only the opponents. Before you go soaring off into the stratosphere, therefore, it's a good idea to have the security of a proven suit fit.

2. *Extra strength.* The opponents will be delighted if their competitive bidding nudges you into a high-level contract that goes down, thus saddling you with a minus score on what should have been a profitable deal for your side. In order to keep them in the doldrums where they belong, be sure to have strength above and beyond what you have already promised before you bid on.

3. *Extra length in your long suit(s).* The more cards you have in your long suits, the better you'll do by declaring and the worse off you'll be if you defend. If you buy the contract, you will enjoy the luxury of a superb trump suit—or, if you have a two-suiter, the powerful playing strength afforded by a long and strong side suit. On defense, however, one of the opponents is sure to be short in view of your length and will quickly ruff in, putting your high cards in such suits to naught. Also, the more freakish the distribution, the more likely it is that both sides can actually *make* their high-level contracts!

4. *Length and weakness in the enemy suit.* If you and your partner have bid spades, both opponents have bid hearts, and you hold ♡ 5 4 3 2, playing the hand is likely to be the winning action. Partner is marked with a void or singleton in hearts and will be able to ruff away most or all of your heart

losers if you play in spades, but your side won't have any trump tricks at all in a heart contract.

5. *Shortness in the enemy suit.* Your high-level contract won't fare very well if the opponents can cash the first three or four tricks. A singleton or void in their bid suit is one good way to prevent such a disaster, and isn't very impressive for defensive purposes. This situation is not as clear-cut as the preceding one, however, for partner just might be looking at several certain tricks in the enemy suit.

Insofar as the vulnerability is concerned, it might seem as though the best time to bid on is when you are vulnerable and the opponents are not. After all, the reward for making game is greater under these conditions, and the bonuses for setting the opponents are smaller. However, there are two important factors that argue in the opposite direction. First, some opponents are so impressed by the same reasoning that they sacrifice even when your game contract would have gone down, and it is decidedly unwise to compound this error by bidding still higher and going down yourself. Second, even if you double and collect only 300 points, you have the consolation of continuing a rubber in which you are well ahead and odds-on to win. Therefore, while the vulnerability is likely to be a good guide as to which side is doing the sacrificing, it is not a reliable clue as to whether or not you should take charge of the auction by bidding.

Let's look at some examples (you are vulnerable):

YOU	LHO	PARTNER	RHO
1 ♡	1 ♠	3 ♡*	4 ♠
?		*13-15 points	

(a)	(b)	(c)
♠ 3	♠ 6	♠ 5 4 3 2
♡ A K J 9 6 2	♡ A Q J 8 3	♡ A K 9 8 3
◇ Q 8 6 3	◇ K Q J 10 4	◇ A Q J 6
♣ K 4	♣ 9 6	♣ —

With hand (a), take control by bidding 5 ♡. Your high hearts will be almost useless on defense, for you can't expect more than one round of the suit to survive the enemy ruffing power. On offense, however, your extra length in hearts and your spade shortness should be worth their weight in gold; and you have enough extra strength to bid at the five-level, for your hand is worth about 17 points in a heart contract and your opening bid promised only 13 or 14.*

A two-suiter like hand (b) is worth a lot of tricks if you declare the contract, but it could easily be a total waste on defense. Thus, you should bid 5 ◊.

The correct bid with hand (c) is not as clear; the important consideration is to rule out either a double or a 5 ♡ bid because your side is almost certain to be cold for slam. The recommended action is to bid 5 ♣, preparing the defense against an eventual spade sacrifice by requesting a club lead, and then make sure that your side reaches at least 6 ♡. The complete deal:

NORTH (partner)
♠ —
♡ Q J 7 6
◊ K 9 4 2
♣ A 6 4 3 2

WEST
♠ A Q J 10 8
♡ 10 5 2
◊ 10
♣ K 8 7 5

EAST
♠ K 9 7 6
♡ 4
◊ 8 7 5 3
♣ Q J 10 9

SOUTH (you)
♠ 5 4 3 2
♡ A K 9 8 3
◊ A Q J 6
♣ — —

*Authorities differ on the exact worth of a hand like (a), but all agree that extra small cards in a long suit that has been supported by partner are worth extra points.

TAKING CHARGE BY DOUBLING

If you have minimal values and the idea of declaring a high-level contract therefore fills you with horror, send a caution signal to your partner by doubling the opponents. This is not a unilateral action, for partner may bid on if he expects to make his contract opposite a minimum hand that may have wasted strength in the enemy suit; but he must have a very good reason in order to overrule your decision. Doubling is likely to be the winning action when you spot the following clues:

1. *A minimum hand for your previous bidding, particularly one that is relatively balanced.* If you have no strength in reserve, it's up to you to warn partner against bidding further—and going down—by doubling. Keep in mind that the more balanced your hand is, the bleaker are your offensive prospects.

2. *Secondary honors in the enemy suit.* Tend to discount a king or queen in the opponents' suit for offensive purposes; such cards won't be worth much if partner turns up with a small singleton. The ace of the enemy suit, however, should be useful for either offense or defense and does *not* indicate that defending will be your best bet.

3. *A probable misfit.* As always, it's best to leave the pain and agony of declaring a misfit to the opponents.

For example, suppose you are vulnerable and the auction proceeds:

YOU	LHO	PARTNER	RHO
1 ♠	Pass	3 ♠	5 ♡
?			

You should double with either of the following hands:

	(a)	♠ K J 7 6 3	(b)	♠ A Q 5 4 2
		♡ 7 4		♡ K J 3
		◇ K Q 10		◇ 7 3
		♣ K J 3		♣ A J 2

Hand (a) is a rock-bottom minimum opening bid, so it is incumbent on you to warn your partner against going on. You should be able to scrounge up at least three defensive tricks, and 5 ♠ could easily turn out to be a disaster.

Hand (b) is stronger, but the secondary honors in the enemy suit tip the scales in favor of defending. Your side's cards might well be:

PARTNER	YOU
♠ K J 8 6	♠ A Q 5 4 2
♡ 7	♡ K J 3
◇ Q J 10 9	◇ 7 3
♣ K Q 9 3	♣ A J 2

Partner will undoubtedly bid 5 ♠ if the decision is left to him. Note the uselessness of your heart honors in a spade contract!

THE FORCING PASS

With a hand that falls between the two previous extremes—namely, one with extra strength but no clear preference between offense and defense—your best strategy is to make a forcing pass and let partner decide what to do. For example (you are vulnerable):

YOU	LHO	PARTNER	RHO
1 ♠	Pass	3 ♠	5 ♡
?			

You hold

♠ A Q 10 7 2
♡ 6 3
◇ K Q 4
♣ A 10 8

You have a better than minimum opening bid, so there is no need to pull the emergency cord by doubling. But you can't

tell whether your side should declare or defend. Partner,
however, may have a strong preference, so pass the decision
around to him. If he has

♠ K J 8 6
♡ Q J 10
◇ J 10 3
♣ K Q J

he'll take a look at his heart strength and unimpressive
distribution and quickly double 5 ♡; while if he holds

♠ K J 8 6
♡ 8
◇ J 10 3
♣ K Q J 9 5

his singleton heart—and the extra strength promised by your
forcing pass—will leave little doubt that a 5 ♠ bid is the
winning action.

Similarly, a forcing pass would have saved my friend from
the sad fate described in the Prologue. He was South and his
side was vulnerable in the following situation:

SOUTH	WEST	NORTH	EAST
1 ♠	4 ♡	4 ♠	5 ♡
?			

He held:

♠ A K 6 5 2
♡ A 7
◇ K 7 3
♣ 7 6 4

His high cards figured to be useful for either offense or
defense and he had no wasted secondary honors in hearts, so his

actual choice of a double was ill-advised—as he learned to his sorrow when he scored only 100 points instead of a vulnerable game. Had he properly made a forcing pass, his partner would have gone on to 5 ♠ holding

♠ Q J 7 3
♡ 6 4
◊ A Q J 5
♣ A 3 2

The forcing pass can also be very useful at a low level of bidding. For example (neither side vulnerable):

YOU	LHO	PARTNER	RHO
1 ♠	Pass	2 ◊	2 ♡
?			

(a) ♠ A K 7 4 3   (b) ♠ A K 7 4 3
     ♡ J 10   ♡ 10 4 2
     ◊ 7 6 2   ◊ A 6
     ♣ A J 9   ♣ A 5 3

It is much too dangerous to double 2 ♡ just to show a minimum opening bid like hand (a), for your right-hand opponent needs only eight tricks to bring home his contract. (In fact, if your side has game, he will register a good sacrifice even if he takes only six or seven tricks.) Hand (b) has extra strength, but no clear preference between offense and defense. Luckily, the auction is forcing, for it can't make sense to sell out to 2 ♡ undoubled after partner's strong two-over-one response, so you should pass in both cases and see what partner chooses to do. As it happens, he has shortness in spades and an excellent penalty double; your side can rack up a lucrative penalty, but has no game. The forcing pass is the only logical way to score a sizeable profit.

One final point should help to avoid a catastrophic misunderstanding: A forcing pass that invites partner to bid at the *seven*-level *guarantees* first-round control of the enemy suit—either the ace or a void. For example (North-South vulnerable):

```
                        NORTH
                        ♠  5 4 2
                        ♡  Q J 8 6 2
                        ◇  10 5
                        ♣  A 8 2
WEST                                              EAST
♠  A 8 3                                          ♠  K Q J 10 9 7 6
♡  10 5 4                                         ♡  K 9 7
◇  8 3                                            ◇  J 4 2
♣  7 6 5 4 3                                      ♣  —
                        SOUTH
                        ♠  —
                        ♡  A 3
                        ◇  A K Q 9 7 6
                        ♣  K Q J 10 9
```

SOUTH	WEST	NORTH	EAST
1 ◇	Pass	1 ♡	3 ♠
6 ♣	Pass	Pass	6 ♠
Pass!	Pass	7 ♣	Pass
Pass	Pass		

South's pass of 6 ♠ is forcing because the nonvulnerable preemptive bidder is obviously sacrificing; it invites North to bid the grand slam, and therefore shows either the ace or a void in spades. North's actual 7 ♣ bid was on the optimistic side, but South, Harold Guiver of Long Beach, California, brought the contract home. He ruffed West's hopeful lead of the ace of spades, crossed to dummy's club ace, and held his breath as he took the heart finesse. When it won, he exhaled, cashed another heart, and started running off the diamonds. Eventually, West had to ruff, whereupon declarer overruffed with dummy's invaluable eight of clubs and drew the rest of West's trumps to score up his grand slam.

NONFORCING AUCTIONS

Keep in mind that an auction is forcing only when it would clearly be absurd to let the opponents play the hand undoubled, as for example when they appear to be sacrificing or when your side can obviously make a contract that is at a much higher level than the one currently under consideration. Don't confuse the previous auctions with one like (opponents are vulnerable):

YOU	LHO	PARTNER	RHO
1 ♡	1 ♠	4 ♡	4 ♠
?			

In view of the vulnerability, your side may well be the one that is sacrificing; and if 5 ♡ looks as though it will be too expensive, you have little choice but to allow the opponents to play in 4 ♠ undoubled. Therefore, a pass by you is *not* forcing. This implies that you must act on your own more often, but a pass is still likely to be your best course if you are in doubt. For example, pass with

♠ 9 8
♡ K J 9 8 3
◇ Q J 9
♣ A K 4

You are neither sure of defeating 4 ♠ nor confident about making 5 ♡, and the opponents could easily hold most of the outstanding strength. Thus, you will not mind if partner also elects to pass. Similarly, the following auctions are not forcing because the opponents may be the ones who hold the balance of power:

(a)	YOU	LHO	PARTNER	RHO
	—	1 ♡	1 ♠	4 ♡
	?			

(b)	YOU	LHO	PARTNER	RHO
	—	—	1 ♠	4 ♡
	?			

There is no reason to believe that your side can make game in either of these examples; your left-hand opponent could have a very strong hand, and you might be broke. Therefore, regardless of the vulnerability, a pass by you is *not* forcing, and partner will be entirely within his rights if he also chooses to pass.

Bidding After a Penalty Double
by Partner

UNILATERAL PENALTY DOUBLES

If you open the bidding with a preempt, a weak two-bid, or a notrump bid, and your partner then doubles an enemy overcall, you have no choice but to pass. Similarly, you are also expected to pass if you make a preemptive or weak jump overcall and partner subsequently doubles the opponents for penalties. The reason for this autocratic state of affairs is that such bids describe your hand very accurately, so partner knows twice as much about your combined holdings as you do. Overruling his decision in spite of his superior knowledge can only lead to a tragedy that would make even a Shakespeare cry:

The Players:

SOUTH: A man with much to learn about unilateral penalty doubles.

WEST: He guessed wrong in a difficult situation, but lived
             to tell about it.
NORTH: His only mistake was partnering South.
EAST: An innocent bystander.
Kibitzers, citizens, soldiers, etc.

The Drama:

> *[A private home. The card room.]*
> *Flourish of trumpets, then hautboys. Enter South,*
> *West, North, and East. South deals and picks up*

$$\spadesuit \quad K \ J \ 9 \ 8 \ 7 \ 6 \ 3$$
$$\heartsuit \quad —$$
$$\diamondsuit \quad 4 \ 3 \ 2$$
$$\clubsuit \quad 10 \ 9 \ 7$$

SOUTH.   "3 ♠. I have a long and strong spade suit and little
              or no defensive strength."
WEST.   "4 ♡. If chance will have me king, why, chance
              may crown me."
KIBITZER.   "He risks it on one turn!"
NORTH.   "Double. What a prospect this opens! What an
              opportunity!"
EAST.   "Pass. All is lost, except a little life."
SOUTH.   "4 ♠. I have a long and strong spade suit and little
              or no defensive strength."
WEST.   "Double. A twice-told tale!"
NORTH.   (to South) "Find yourself a partner!"
Exit North. Alarums and Excursions. Exeunt.
                           Finis

Just for the record, North held:

$$\spadesuit \quad 10$$
$$\heartsuit \quad A \ J \ 10 \ 9 \ 2$$
$$\diamondsuit \quad A \ K \ 9$$
$$\clubsuit \quad Q \ J \ 6 \ 5$$

If instead you open with a strong two-bid and partner doubles an overcall, you do have some leeway, for you may pull the double if you have game in your own hand. For example, if you open with a strong 2 ♡ bid (or a strong and artificial 2 ♣ bid), your left-hand opponent overcalls 2 ♠, and partner doubles, you may remove to 4 ♡ if you hold

          ♠   3
          ♡   A K Q J 10 9 7
          ◇   A K 8
          ♣   A 9

Be sure to pass, however, with any hand that does not guarantee game opposite a virtual Yarborough.

DOUBLES OF LOW-LEVEL SUIT OVERCALLS

If you open the bidding with one of a suit and partner then doubles a two-level overcall for penalties, you are expected to cooperate in the final decision. This opening bid covers a wide range of point counts and distributions, so partner isn't much more knowledgeable about your combined holdings than you are. His penalty double is more than just a vague hint, so your best course will often be to leave it alone. But it is essential to watch for those signals that indicate it is time to overrule his decision. These include:

1. *Fewer than three defensive tricks.* It is desirable to have at least three defensive tricks in order to sit for partner's low-level penalty double, for he is expecting a fair amount of help from you in view of your opening one-bid.

2. *A long and strong side suit.* As usual, you are likely to be better off on offense if you have a two-suited hand.

3. *A void in trumps.* Partner isn't expecting you to show up with much in the way of trump tricks, but he is hoping that you will have a small trump or two so that you can lead through declarer. This will enable your side to cut down any ruffing power that dummy may have without partner having to lead away from his trump honors, and it also makes a fatal endplay

by declarer less likely. Obviously, it will be quite difficult for you to cooperate with this intelligent battle plan if you don't have any trumps at all!*

4. *A weak bid suit that you don't want partner to lead.* Partner's penalty double is based in part on shortness in the suit in which you have opened, and indicates that he will probably lead it in the hope of getting some tricks (and some ruffs). This plan is likely to work well if your suit is respectable, especially if it includes the ace; but if you happen to have bid on J 9 8 7 3, his lead will not work out in the way that he expects. This will not necessarily be fatal; but it does suggest that in close situations, you should decide in favor of an escape if you aren't looking forward to an opening lead in your bid suit.

5. *A reasonable escape spot.* If the only way you can pull partner's double is by making a horrible bid, such as rebidding a weak suit in the face of partner's promised shortness, you might as well take your chances on defeating the opponents.

Let's look at some examples (both sides vulnerable):

YOU	LHO	PARTNER	RHO
1 ♠	2 ◊	Double*	Pass
?		*Penalties	

(a) ♠ A K 8 7 3
   ♡ A 9 5
   ◊ 6
   ♣ Q 4 3 2

Pass. Your defensive strength is adequate, a spade lead is just what you want, and you can lead a round of trumps through declarer if necessary.

---

*A void in trumps is not as much of a drawback against a declarer of modest skill who is unlikely to execute an endplay, and who may suffer a nervous breakdown (and drop numerous extra tricks) when he discovers that the trumps have split 5-0.

(b) ♠ A 9 7 4 3
     ♡ A J 3
     ◇ J 10
     ♣ K 10 2

Pass. You have only two and a half defensive tricks, but the diamond honors offer some compensation; and no escape is attractive.

(c) ♠ K Q J 8 6 2
     ♡ K Q 8
     ◇ 7
     ♣ Q 4 3

Bid 2 ♠. Your defensive strength is below par, so there is too much danger that 2 ◇ doubled will make. Of course, partner might have four trump tricks and a side ace or two, but it is losing strategy to use this penalty double as a unilateral action.

(d) ♠ J 9 7 6 3
     ♡ A K 8 4 2
     ◇ 6
     ♣ A 8

Bid 2 ♡. Partner could easily be long in hearts, which would be excellent for offensive purposes but fatal if you defend. Also, you aren't happy about the idea of a spade lead.

(e) ♠ K 10 8 7 5
     ♡ A J 7 2
     ◇ —
     ♣ K 7 4 3

Bid 2 ♡. With only two defensive tricks and a void in the enemy suit, your hand isn't very suitable for defending.

(f) ♠ A K Q 8 6
     ♡ K 10 7 6
     ◇ —
     ♣ K Q 6 2

Bid 3 ◇. Your defensive strength is impressive, but your offensive prospects are even better. The cue-bid lets partner know that you are running not out of fright, but because you expect to score the most points by declaring game or slam.

If instead you are using negative doubles, your strategy is essentially similar. Partner passes 2 ◊ instead of doubling; you protect him by doubling with hands (a) and (b), but make exactly the same bids as shown with the other four hands.

DOUBLES OF HIGH-LEVEL SUIT OVERCALLS

If you open the bidding with one of a suit and partner doubles a preemptive overcall for penalties, pass unless your hand is very freakish. You only need a few tricks to defeat the enemy contract, and it is very risky to start shopping around for a fit at a high level of bidding. Thus, you will usually do best by playing for the penalty. Keep in mind that the higher the level at which partner doubles, the less you are expected to cooperate in the decision.

DOUBLES OF NOTRUMP BIDS

Notrump overcalls. If you open the bidding with one of a suit, your left-hand opponent overcalls with 1 NT, and partner doubles, it's not advisable to run unless your hand is very distributional. After all, your left-hand opponent has at least 16 points *and* strength in the suit that you have bid, so any bid by you is likely to evoke a lethal penalty double. Furthermore, the auction suggests that declarer will be presented with a barren dummy and suffer the embarrassment of having to lead away from the high cards in his hand. Therefore, an escape is likely to be right only if you have a shapely hand with a minimum in high cards like

♠ A J 10 6 3
♡ K Q J 9 8
◊ 3
♣ 4 2

1 NT opening bids. If your left-hand opponent opens with 1 NT and partner doubles, don't run unless you have a weak hand with a long suit. For example, escape to 2 ♠ with

♠ Q J 7 6 5 3
♡ —
◇ 7 2
♣ 8 6 5 4 3

With a balanced hand, you are likely to get your best result by passing even if you have a Yarborough; any contract of your own will probably fare badly in view of your pitiful assets and left-hand opponent's strength, and partner should have a fair chance of defeating 1 NT in his own hand. And if your hand is somewhat stronger, like

♠ A Q 8 6 4
♡ 7 2
◇ 6 5 3
♣ J 10 8

1 NT is undoubtedly in terrible trouble. Partner should have at least 16 points, so you can place your opponents with probable counts of 16 and 0—numbers that are likely to give rise to far more attractive ones, such as 500 or 700 on your side of the score sheet.

Review Quiz

In each of the following problems, the vulnerability and bidding are shown. What call do you make?

(1)   You are vulnerable

YOU	LHO	PARTNER	RHO
1 ♠	4 ♡	4 ♠	5 ♡
?			

You hold:
♠ A Q 10 3 2
♡ 3 2
◇ A Q
♣ A 10 9 7

(2)   You are vulnerable

YOU	LHO	PARTNER	RHO
1 ♡	4 ♠	5 ♡	6 ♠
?			

You hold:
♠ 2
♡ A K Q 8 6 5
◇ A 10 3
♣ K Q 5

(3)   Opponents are vulnerable

YOU	LHO	PARTNER	RHO
1 ♡	2 ♣	4 ♡	5 ♣
?			

You hold:
♠ A 6 2
♡ K 10 8 7 3
◇ A 10 7
♣ A 4

(4) You are vulnerable

YOU	LHO	PARTNER	RHO	You hold:
1 ♠	4 ♡	4 ♠	5 ♡	♠ K Q 10 7 4 2
?				♡ —
				◇ A J 8 6
				♣ K 10 8

(5) You are vulnerable

YOU	LHO	PARTNER	RHO	You hold:
1 ♡	1 ♠	3 ♡*	4 ♠	♠ 4 3
?				♡ K J 8 7 5
		*13-15 points		◇ A 6 3
				♣ K Q 2

(6) Both sides vulnerable

YOU	LHO	PARTNER	RHO	You hold:
1 ♠	Pass	2 ♡	3 ◇	♠ A K 8 6 2
?				♡ Q 6
				◇ 8 5
				♣ A Q 9 7

(7) You are vulnerable

YOU	LHO	PARTNER	RHO	You hold:
—	—	1 ♡	1 ♠	♠ K 8 3
3 ♡*	4 ♠	Pass	Pass	♡ A 9 7 6
?				◇ Q J 10
	* 13-15 points			♣ K 5 2

(8)   You are vulnerable

YOU	LHO	PARTNER	RHO	You hold:
—	—	1 ♡	1 ♠	♠ 7
3 ♡*	4 ♠	Pass	Pass	♡ K Q 8 6
?				◇ A 10 9 7
		* 13-15 points		♣ Q 10 8 6

(9)   You are vulnerable

YOU	LHO	PARTNER	RHO	You hold:
1 ♠	4 ♡	Pass	Pass	♠ A K 8 6 3
?				♡ K 5 2
				◇ K 4 3
				♣ 10 8

(10) Neither side vulnerable

YOU	LHO	PARTNER	RHO	You hold:
1 ♡	2 ♣	Double*	Pass	♠ A 7 3
?				♡ A K 8 6 4 3
		* Penalties		◇ K J 4
				♣ 7

(11) Neither side vulnerable

YOU	LHO	PARTNER	RHO	You hold:
3 ♡	4 ◇	Double	Pass	♠ Q J 10
?				♡ Q J 10 9 7 6 4
				◇ —
				♣ 4 3 2

(12) Both sides vulnerable

YOU	LHO	PARTNER	RHO
1 ♠	2 ♣	Double*	Pass
?

* Penalties

You hold:
- ♠ Q 9 7 6 3
- ♡ A K Q J 4
- ♢ 5 3
- ♣ 2

(13) Both sides vulnerable

YOU	LHO	PARTNER	RHO
1 ♠	2 ♣	Double*	Pass
?

*Penalties

You hold:
- ♠ K 10 6 4 3
- ♡ K 7 4 2
- ♢ A J 8 7
- ♣ ——

(14) Both sides vulnerable

YOU	LHO	PARTNER	RHO
1 ♠	4 ♣	Double	Pass
?

You hold:
- ♠ K 10 6 4 3
- ♡ K 7 4 2
- ♢ A J 8 7
- ♣ ——

(15) Both sides vulnerable

YOU	LHO	PARTNER	RHO
—	1 NT*	Double	Pass
?

* 16-18 points

You hold:
- ♠ J 8 6 3
- ♡ 7 2
- ♢ 10 8 5 3
- ♣ J 9 7

Solutions

1. *Pass.* Partner's hand is shrouded in mystery; he may have been stretching to bid 4 ♠, or he may have been close to a slam try. Fortunately, there is no need to put your ESP to the test; a forcing pass, showing more strength than you have already promised and no clear preference between offense and defense, will enable partner to make a well-informed decision.

2. *Double.* You have enough overall strength for a forcing pass, but you cannot invite partner to bid a grand slam unless you have first-round control of the enemy suit.

3. *Double.* This auction is not forcing, so increase the probable penalty while you can.

4. *Five spades.* You belong on offense even if partner stretched to bid 4 ♠. His hand:

   ♠   A J 6 5
   ♡   8 4 2
   ◇   7 5 3
   ♣   A Q J

5. *Double.* You have a minimum opening bid, so you must warn partner against going on to 5 ♡.

6. *Pass.* Partner may have an excellent penalty double, and you have no idea where the hand belongs. Give him a chance to do his thing. The auction is forcing, so you are assured of another chance to speak.

7. *Double.* The auction is forcing, so you can't pass, and a five-level contract is highly inadvisable in view of your balanced minimum.

8. *Five hearts.* Your singleton spade and the extra strength promised by partner's forcing pass argue strongly in favor of bidding on. Change the heart queen to the ace and you should try for slam by cue-bidding 5 ◇.

9. *Pass.* This auction is not forcing.
10. *Pass.* You have excellent defensive strength and will welcome a heart lead.
11. *Pass.* Beware of Shakespearean tragedies! After you have preempted, partner's penalty double is an absolute and inviolable command to pass.
12. *Two hearts.* If partner has length in hearts, which is likely, most of your high-card strength will be totally wasted on defense.
13. *Two diamonds.* Don't sit for a *low*-level penalty double with a void in the enemy suit and limited defensive strength.
14. *Pass.* Don't pull a double of a *high*-level suit overcall unless your hand is very freakish. You have no reason to believe that your side can make a four-level contract; in fact, had partner passed 4 ♣, you would also have passed. Therefore, it hardly makes sense to bid now that he has announced that he expects to defeat the enemy contract.
15. *Pass.* Bidding is likely to prove fatal in view of your terrible hand and left-hand opponent's strength, and partner may be able to defeat 1 NT all by himself. Even if he can't, it's better to let the opponents make 1 NT doubled than to suffer a set of 500 or 800 points.

6

Lead-Directing Doubles

♠ ♡ ◇ ♣

If today's high cost of living causes a serious decline in your finances, you might consider visiting your friendly neighborhood loan company. A better plan, however, is to schedule an evening of bridge against opponents who are quick to double slam contracts in order to increase the prospective penalty.

```
                         NORTH
                         ♠  K 10 9
                         ♡  A K Q 10 8 4
                         ◇  Q J 10
                         ♣  J
    WEST                                      EAST
    ♠  7 6 4 3                                ♠  8 5 2
    ♡  9 5 2                                  ♡  7 6 3
    ◇  7 6 4 3                                ◇  A K 2
    ♣  8 4                                    ♣  6 5 3 2
                         SOUTH
                         ♠  A Q J
                         ♡  J
                         ◇  9 8 5
                         ♣  A K Q 10 9 7
```

SOUTH	WEST	NORTH	EAST
—	—	1 ♡	Pass
3 ♣	Pass	3 ♡	Pass
4 ♣	Pass	4 NT	Pass
5 ♡	Pass	6 NT	Double?
7 ♣ !	Pass	Pass	Pass

North and South were about to stop in a hopeless 6 NT contract, but East came to their rescue by making a greedy double. South, being no fool, realized that his side had committed a faux pas during the bidding and ran out to 7 ♣, which had the advantage of placing West on lead. After some *very* agonized thought, West led a spade. East's arithmetical talent was sadly lacking; in order to try and increase the penalty by 50 points, he handed his opponents a 1,440-point bonanza.

Doubles in Slam Auctions

DOUBLES OF SLAM CONTRACTS

Doubling a slam contract simply to increase the prospective penalty is usually a poor idea, for several reasons. First, the opponents are unlikely to go down more than one trick in view of their great power, so you stand to gain only 50 or 100 points by your double; but you are risking the loss of several hundred points if the opponents make their contract, and even more if they redouble. Second, if you double a suit slam on high-card strength, such as two aces or ace-king in a side suit, the opponents may well turn up with a critical void or singleton and easily make their contract. Third, the information given declarer by the double will often help him find the play that saves the contract, as my friend discovered in the example given in the Prologue when he doubled 6 ♠ holding ♠ Q J 10 8, only to fall victim to a cleverly executed endplay. Fourth, the double will cost well over 1000 points if the opponents take heed and run to a different slam that they can make, as in the case described at the beginning of this chapter.

A much better strategy is to double a slam contract in order to suggest a particular opening lead to your partner, a lead you think is essential to defeat the slam. Now you stand to gain not just 50 or 100 points, but the entire value of the slam that the opponents will be prevented from making. The best procedure is the one developed by Theodore Lightner, in which the double is used to request an *unusual lead*. The most frequent meaning of the Lightner double is that the doubler is void in a side suit and wishes an immediate ruff, so the opening leader should look with favor on his longest nontrump suit. A trump lead is barred, as is any suit bid by you. If he is in doubt, he should lead the first side suit bid by dummy or, if dummy doesn't happen to have bid a side suit, the first nontrump suit bid by declarer. For example:

YOU	LHO	PARTNER	RHO
—	1 ♡	Pass	3 ♡
Pass	4 NT	Pass	5 ♡
Pass	6 ♡	Pass	Pass
?			

You hold:

♠ 10 6 5 4 2
♡ A 7 4
♢ —
♣ 8 6 4 3 2

You should double, asking partner to look around for a suit that you can ruff on the opening lead. The complete deal:

NORTH
♠ A Q J
♡ 10 9 3 2
♢ A Q 5
♣ 10 9 5

WEST (partner)
♠ 9 8 7
♡ 6
♢ 8 7 6 4 3 2
♣ K Q J

EAST (you)
♠ 10 6 5 4 2
♡ A 7 4
♢ —
♣ 8 6 4 3 2

SOUTH
♠ K 3
♡ K Q J 8 5
♢ K J 10 9
♣ A 7

Without your double, partner would undoubtedly lead the king of clubs, and South would wrap up his slam by simply playing three rounds of spades and pitching his club loser before driving out the ace of trumps.

At times, it is desirable to take advantage of the fact that if partner is in doubt about which suit your double requests, he should turn his attention to dummy's first-bid side suit:

YOU	LHO	PARTNER	RHO
—	1 ♡	Pass	2 ♣
Pass	2 ◇	Pass	2 ♠
Pass	3 ◇	Pass	3 ♡
Pass	6 ♡	Pass	Pass
?			

You hold:

$$♠ \quad 9 \ 7 \ 4 \ 3$$
$$♡ \quad Q \ J \ 10$$
$$◇ \quad 8 \ 4 \ 2$$
$$♣ \quad A \ 6 \ 5$$

You should double. Ordinarily, it is best to try and set up a side-suit winner before declarer establishes some discards by knocking out your ace in dummy's suit. Here, however, the auction suggests that declarer holds 6-5 distribution in the red suits, so he may discard his club losers on dummy's high spades if the suit is not led at once.

See if you can spot the lead requested by the double in the following auction:

YOU	LHO	PARTNER	RHO
—	1 ♡	Pass	3 ♡
Pass	4 ♣	Pass	4 ♡
Pass	6 ♡	Pass	Pass
Double	Pass	Pass	Pass

Either of the unbid suits would be a relatively normal lead, so—unless partner has a very long suit that he thinks you want to ruff—a club is his indicated choice.

As you can see, lead-directing doubles can be extremely effective. Of course, it is essential that partner be on the same wavelength, so don't spring one on him without prior discussion, unless he is an expert. Also, if the opponents are likely to escape to a slam contract that you cannot defeat, you should simply pass and hope that partner happens to select the suit you want:

YOU	LHO	PARTNER	RHO
—	—	—	1 ♣
Pass	2 ♠	Pass	3 ♦
Pass	3 NT	Pass	6 ♠
?			

You hold:

♠ 8 7
♡ K J 9 8 3
♦ J 9 8 7 6 3
♣ —

You very much want a club lead against 6 ♠, and a double will probably get it for you—if the opponents stay there. However, your left-hand opponent has already made one suggestion about playing in notrump, and you have very poor defense against a 6 NT contract. Therefore, your only real chance to register a set is a discreet pass. The complete deal:

NORTH
- ♠ Q 10 5 3 2
- ♡ 7
- ◇ A K 10
- ♣ A J 8 3

WEST
- ♠ K 6
- ♡ 10 6 5 4 2
- ◇ 5 2
- ♣ 10 9 6 5

EAST
- ♠ 8 7
- ♡ K J 9 8 3
- ◇ J 9 8 7 6 3
- ♣ —

SOUTH
- ♠ A J 9 4
- ♡ A Q
- ◇ Q 4
- ♣ K Q 7 4 2

Unlikely as it may seem from the following discussion, this remarkable example is from the 1960 World Championship Olympiad. North started things off on a bizarre note by opening with 1 ♣ because one of his spades was in with his clubs, a fact he happened to discover on the second round of bidding. East's pass to 6 ♠ was more sensible; had he made a lead-directing double, both opponents would have probably run out to the laydown 6 NT contract. Unfortunately for his side, West led a diamond. South could now have clinched his contract by playing the ace and another trump, but he won the opening lead in dummy and *took the spade finesse.* West joined in the general confusion by seizing his king of trumps and returning—a *diamond!* So South scored up his slam; and East could do nothing but explain to his partner in no uncertain terms the meaning of his play of the three of diamonds at trick one.

When the deal was replayed in the other room, North survived the first pitfall by arranging his hand correctly. It was not long, however, before he fell from grace; his side also bypassed the two ice-cold slam contracts and wound up in 6 ♠, and he (as declarer) won East's opening heart lead and crossed to his hand in order to take the spade finesse. West instigated a return to sanity by winning with his king and returning a club, giving East the ruff that beat the slam—and his team just enough of a gain to eke out a win in the match.

DOUBLES OF CUE-BIDS

If the opponents are cue-bidding merrily in an attempt to reach slam, you can often illuminate the best lead by using a lead-directing double of a cue-bid as a signal flare. For example:

YOU	LHO	PARTNER	RHO
—	1 ♠	Pass	3 ♠
Pass	4 ♣	Pass	4 ◇
Double	4 ♠	Pass	6 ♠
Pass	Pass	Pass	

The 4 ◇ bid is not an attempt to play the hand in diamonds. It is intended to help the opponents investigate their slam chances, and presumably shows the ace or another important feature. You can tell that the most likely result of the auction is an eventual spade contract, in which case partner will be on lead, so you should double 4 ◇ to ask him to lead a diamond if you have a hand like

```
♠  7 3
♡  6 4 2
◇  K Q 10 8
♣  5 4 3 2
```

However, *don't* double 4 ◇ with

```
♠  7 6 3
♡  K 8 5
◇  K 7 3
♣  8 6 4 2
```

For all you know, a heart may be the killing lead. Even if the heart king is changed to a small heart, the double is still wrong, for partner might have the king-queen of hearts and be able to establish the setting trick by leading that suit before your king of diamonds is driven out and declarer takes some discards on dummy's suit. An additional reason to avoid doubling a cue-bid in close cases is that it allows your left-hand opponent two additional bids, redouble and pass, to further define his holding; and this chance to exchange information may be all the opponents need to arrive at the best contract. Furthermore, your double of a cue-bid may give an expert declarer just the information he needs to make a difficult contract:

NORTH
♠ A K J
♡ 5 4
♢ K 6 4 3
♣ A Q 7 6

WEST
♠ 8 5 4
♡ A 10 9 6 2
♢ 10 8
♣ 10 8 3

EAST
♠ 2
♡ J 8 3
♢ Q 9 7 2
♣ K J 9 5 2

SOUTH
♠ Q 10 9 7 6 3
♡ K Q 7
♢ A J 5
♣ 4

SOUTH	WEST	NORTH	EAST
—	—	1 NT	Pass
3 ♠	Pass	4 ♣	Double
4 ♢	Pass	4 ♠	Pass
5 ♣	Pass	5 ♢	Pass
6 ♠	Pass	Pass	Pass

This deal helped the team of B. J. Becker, Michael Becker, Andy Bernstein, and Jeff Rubens win the coveted 1972 U.S. Summer National Knockout Team Championship. North's 4 ♣ bid showed a maximum hand with spade support and a club feature. Had East left it alone, South might well have gone down. Rather than risk the whole hand on the diamond finesse, it is tempting to cash the ace and king of diamonds and then, if the queen fails to drop, take the club finesse in order to dispose of the diamond loser. As you can see, this line fails, as the declarer in the other room found to his regret when he tried it.

After East's telltale double, however, South (B. J. Becker) knew that the club finesse would not succeed, so he embarked on a different plan. He won the opening club lead with dummy's ace and played a heart to his king; West won with the ace and returned a heart. South won with the queen, ruffed a heart with dummy's king of spades, ruffed a club, played a spade to the ace, ruffed another club with the nine of spades, and drew trumps. With four cards left, the position was:

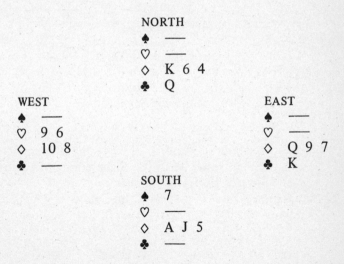

NORTH
♠ —
♡ —
◊ K 6 4
♣ Q

WEST
♠ —
♡ 9 6
◊ 10 8
♣ —

EAST
♠ —
♡ —
◊ Q 9 7
♣ K

SOUTH
♠ 7
♡ —
◊ A J 5
♣ —

With a lot of points at stake, South naturally wished to spare himself the guess as to whether to finesse in diamonds or try to drop the doubleton queen in the West hand, and he did so by leading his last trump and pitching a diamond from dummy. East also had to discard a diamond. When South now led a diamond to dummy's king and returned a diamond, he was able to see East's last diamond before making his decision—and he could not possibly go wrong.

It's also a poor idea to double a cue-bid for purposes of lead direction when the opponents may be able to play in that suit. Don't commit the mortifying error that an opponent of mine once made:

SOUTH	WEST	NORTH	EAST
1 ◇	Pass	1 ♡	Pass
4 ♡	Pass	5 ♣	Pass
5 ◇	Double	Pass	Pass
Redouble!	Pass	Pass	Pass

West wanted a diamond lead, which he would ruff, against a 5 ♡ or 6 ♡ contract; and this plan would in fact have resulted in a set. Unfortunately for his side, however, the bidding never got that far, for as South, I held ◇ A Q J 10 4 3 and was more than willing to play the cold redoubled contract in the suit in which I had opened the bidding.

DOUBLES OF BLACKWOOD RESPONSES

A new-suit bid in response to the Blackwood convention is similar to a cue-bid in that the opponents are unlikely to be able to play the hand in that suit, so you can double if you want to tell partner what to lead. For example:

YOU	LHO	PARTNER	RHO
—	1 ♡	Pass	3 ♡
Pass	4 NT	Pass	5 ◇
Double	6 ♡	Pass	Pass
Pass			

The double shows a very strong preference for a diamond lead, such as

♠ 7 3
♡ 6 4 2
♢ K Q 10 8
♣ 5 4 3 2

Sometimes you can specify the lead of any of the three nontrump suits by judicious use of lead-directing doubles. For example:

YOU	LHO	PARTNER	RHO
–	1 ♠	Pass	2 ♡
Pass	3 ♠	Pass	4 ♠
Pass	4 NT	Pass	5 ♢
?			

(a)	(b)	(c)
♠ A 4 2	♠ A 4 2	♠ A 4 2
♡ J 10 7 4 2	♡ —	♡ J 10 7 4 2
♢ —	♢ J 10 7 4 2	♢ J 10 9 7 3
♣ J 10 9 7 3	♣ J 10 9 7 3	♣ —

The opponents are likely to wind up in 6 ♠, so you should begin planning now in order to obtain the ruff that will defeat their slam. With hand (a), all you need do is double 5 ♢ and *not* double the final contract. If you have hand (b), passing 5 ♢ and then doubling 6 ♠ will suggest the lead of the first side suit bid by dummy. And with hand (c), you can double 5 ♢ *and* double 6 ♠ in order to call for the suit that you could not insist upon by either of the preceding methods—clubs.*

*All doubles of slam contracts are assumed to be lead-directional, so the double of 6 ♠ is best treated as part of an overall message and *not* as an attempt to increase the penalty. This procedure is not as well known as the preceding two, however, so it's a good idea to check it out with your partner before you try it at the bridge table.

DOUBLES AFTER PARTNER HAS
DOUBLED A BLACKWOOD RESPONSE

On occasion, you may encounter an auction like:

YOU	LHO	PARTNER	RHO
—	—	—	1 ♣
Pass	1 ◇	Pass	1 ♠
Pass	2 NT	Pass	3 ♣
Pass	4 ♣	Pass	4 NT
Pass	5 ♡	Double	6 NT
?			

You hold:

♠ J 10 4 3
♡ Q 4 2
◇ 8 7 4 2
♣ A 3

Partner's double of 5 ♡ requested a heart lead against
what seemed to be a probable club contract, but the auction
took a surprising turn: *He* will be on lead against 6 NT. If he has
the king of hearts, a heart lead will set up a second winner
before your club ace is driven out and will probably defeat the
slam, but partner may be afraid to lead away from his honor.
Therefore, you should double 6 NT, which confirms that the
suit suggested by partner's double is still best even though the
lead will be coming from his side of the table.

Doubles of Strongly Bid Game Contracts

Doubles of strongly bid game contracts also possess lead-directional implications, particularly when the final contract is 3 NT.

DOUBLES AFTER 1 NT/3 NT

We have seen that it is generally losing strategy to double 3 NT simply because you hold a scattering of high cards. Declarer's task is always much easier when the defensive strength is concentrated in one hand, especially when he is alerted to this fact by a double. He knows which finesses will win and which will lose, and is usually able to subject the doubler to such indignities as endplays (because his partner is broke and can never gain the lead), squeezes (because he holds all the high cards and declarer's side must have tricks somewhere, such as a long suit), and writing down large numbers on declarer's side of the score sheet (because of his foolish double). Therefore, the best strategy with such hands is to lie low and pass.

As a result, if your left-hand opponent opens with 1 NT and your right-hand opponent raises to 3 NT, a double is best used to request an unusual lead with a hand like

♠ K Q J 10 9
♡ 7 6 3
◇ A 4 2
♣ 3 2

or

♠   7 3
♡   8 4 2
♦   A K Q J 10 8
♣   4 3

While partner does not know exactly which suit to lead, he should guess right most of the time if he selects his *shortest* one. Without the double, partner would probably make a mundane lead such as the fourth best from his longest and strongest suit, which is surely *not* the one you want, and declarer might easily be able to run off nine tricks before your side could collect five.

DOUBLES OF STRONGLY BID 3 NT CONTRACTS

Doubles of 3 NT contracts reached by auctions other than 1 NT/3 NT usually have some lead-directional implications, although the doubler's basic goal may be to increase the penalty.

1. *Your side has not bid a suit.* If you and your partner have not bid any suits, a double suggests the lead of the suit first bid by dummy (unless it has been rebid several times). An example was given in Chapter 4.

2. *Only partner has bid a suit.* If only partner has bid a suit and you ultimately double 3 NT, you are insisting that he lead his suit. The occasion for this double arises when you hold a high honor or two in partner's suit and know that the opponents' stopper is shaky or nonexistent, but fear that their no-trump bidding will persuade partner to make a different lead. A world-famous pair went wrong by neglecting this principle in the following deal, which is taken from the 1962 Trials to select the U.S. International Team:

                    NORTH
                    ♠ A 4
                    ♡ A K Q 9 7 6
                    ◇ Q 6 2
                    ♣ 4 3

WEST   EAST
♠ J 7 5 3   ♠ K Q 2
♡ J 2   ♡ 10 4 3
◇ 10 9   ◇ K 7 5 4
♣ A J 8 5 2   ♣ K Q 7

                    SOUTH
                    ♠ 10 9 8 6
                    ♡ 8 5
                    ◇ A J 8 3
                    ♣ 10 9 6

SOUTH	WEST	NORTH	EAST
—	Pass	1 ♡	Double
1 NT	2 ♣	3 NT	Double
Pass	Pass	Pass	

East doubled 3 NT to tell West to ignore the enemy bluff (or confusion) and lead his own suit. West, however, led a spade, whereupon South had no trouble fulfilling his doubled contract.

If only partner has bid a suit and *he* doubles 3 NT, and you are on lead, you must lead his suit unless you are void.

3. *Only you have bid a suit.* Similar reasoning applies if only you have bid a suit. A double by partner asks you to lead your suit, while a double by you insists that partner lead the suit that you have bid.

4. *Both you and your partner have bid different suits.* If

both you and your partner have bid different suits and the partner of the opening leader doubles 3 NT, the opening leader should lead his own suit. This situation is not as clear as the preceding ones, however, so you should check it out in advance with your partner to be sure you are playing it the same way.

THE FISHER DOUBLE

Dr. John W. Fisher has devised a lead-directing double that applies when the opponents open the bidding with 1 NT and subsequently play in 3 NT. If they have *not* used a Stayman 2 ♣ response, a double of the final contract requests a club lead. If they *have* used a Stayman, a double of the final contract requests a diamond lead. The main advantage of this convention is that the opening leader knows exactly what is expected of him, so there is no possibility of ambiguity. The disadvantages are that after the auction 1 NT/3 NT, the Lightner double can be used regardless of what suit you want led and is therefore preferable with a capable partner who will judge correctly most of the time; and the Fisher double implies that doubles of Stayman 2 ♣ bids should be used as lead-directional, which (as we will see in Chapter 8) is *not* a recommended procedure.

DOUBLES OF STRONGLY BID SUIT GAMES

On rare occasions, a lead-directional double of a strongly bid suit game will reap rich dividends. For example:

YOU	LHO	PARTNER	RHO
—	—	—	1 ◇
Pass	1 ♡	Pass	4 ♡
?			

You hold:

    ♠ J 6
    ♡ A K 3
    ◇ A Q 3
    ♣ 8 7 6 4 2

The opponents' bidding is full of vim and vigor, so a penalty double is unlikely to be the winning action. Therefore, a double is lead-directional, suggesting the unusual lead of the first side suit bid by dummy. Dummy is marked with most of the missing strength by his triple raise to 4 ♡, so he should have the diamond king, and partner may never again be on lead. Therefore, a diamond lead at trick one may well be the only way to defeat the contract.

Here's an example suggested by well-known expert and theorist Marshall Miles:

YOU	LHO	PARTNER	RHO
—	—	—	1 ◇
3 ♠	4 ♡	4 ♠	5 ♡
?			

You hold:

    ♠ K Q J 10 7 6 3
    ♡ 7 2
    ◇ 6 5 4 3
    ♣ —

Since the partner of a preemptive bidder is always in charge of the auction, a double by you would be decidedly odd—and therefore a Lightner double. The complete deal might well be:

NORTH
- ♠ 9 4
- ♡ K 10 8 6
- ◇ A K Q 8 7
- ♣ Q 5

WEST (partner)
- ♠ A 8 2
- ♡ 4 3
- ◇ J 2
- ♣ K 8 6 4 3 2

EAST (you)
- ♠ K Q J 10 7 6 3
- ♡ 7 2
- ◇ 6 5 4 3
- ♣ —

SOUTH
- ♠ 5
- ♡ A Q J 9 5
- ◇ 10 9
- ♣ A J 10 9 7

A club lead and ruff, spade to the ace, and another club ruff is the only way to defeat the 5 ♡ contract.

Review Quiz

In each of the following problems, both sides are vulnerable, and the auction proceeds as shown. What call do you make?

(1)

YOU	LHO	PARTNER	RHO	You hold:
—	1 ♠	Pass	2 NT	♠ A 7 3
Pass	3 ♠	Pass	4 ♠	♡ —
Pass	4 NT	Pass	5 ♠	◇ 8 6 5 4 3
Pass	6 ♠	Pass	Pass	♣ K Q 4 3 2
?				

(2)

YOU	LHO	PARTNER	RHO	You hold:
—	1 ♡	Pass	1 ♠	♠ 8 5 4 3 2
Pass	3 ◇	Pass	3 ♡	♡ 7 6 3
Pass	4 NT	Pass	5 ◇	◇ 10 6 4 3 2
Pass	6 ♡	Pass	Pass	♣ —
?				

(3)

YOU	LHO	PARTNER	RHO	You hold:
—	1 ♠	2 ◇	2 ♡	♠ A 6 2
Pass	3 ♠	Pass	4 ◇	♡ 7 5 4 3
?				◇ —
				♣ 9 8 6 4 3 2

(4)

YOU	LHO	PARTNER	RHO	You hold:
1 ♡	Double	Pass	3 ♣	♠ A 7 3
Pass	3 ♠	Pass	4 ♠	♡ A K J 4 2
Pass	6 ♠	Pass	Pass	◇ 5 3
?				♣ 4 3 2

(5)	YOU	LHO	PARTNER	RHO	You hold:
	—	1 ♠	Pass	3 ♠	♠ 7 6 3
	Pass	4 NT	Pass	5 ◇	♡ A 8 2
	?				◇ K Q J 2
					♣ 4 3 2

(6)	YOU	LHO	PARTNER	RHO	You hold:
	—	1 ♠	Pass	3 ♠	♠ 7 6 3
	Pass	4 NT	Pass	5 ◇	♡ K 8 5
	?				◇ K 8 5
					♣ 7 6 4 2

(7)	YOU	LHO	PARTNER	RHO	You hold:
	1 ♡	1 ♠	2 ♡	3 ♡	♠ A K 3
	Pass	4 ◇	Pass	6 ◇	♡ Q J 9 7 4
	?				◇ 4
					♣ J 9 8 6

(8)	YOU	LHO	PARTNER	RHO	You hold:
	—	1 NT	Pass	3 NT	♠ A 3 2
	?				♡ 5 4
					◇ K Q J 10 9 2
					♣ 4 2

(9)	YOU	LHO	PARTNER	RHO	You hold:
	—	1 NT	Pass	3 NT	♠ Q 6
	?				♡ A Q J 8 7
					◇ 10 8 3
					♣ K 4 2

(10) YOU	LHO	PARTNER	RHO	You hold:
—	1 NT	2 ♠	3 NT	♠ K J 3
?				♡ J 9 5 4 3
				◇ 2
				♣ 7 6 4 3

Solutions

1. *Double.* Alert partner to the desirability of trying for an immediate ruff at trick one. His longest side suit is almost surely hearts, and the opponents will not enjoy an escape to 6 NT after your lead of the club king.

2. *Pass.* The normal lead of the unbid club suit is just what you want, and a double might steer partner away from it. To make matters worse, you have no defense whatsoever against a 6 NT contract.

3. *Double.* You would have raised on the previous round in order to show diamond support, so the sole purpose of this double is to request a diamond lead against an eventual spade contract by the enemy.

4. *Pass.* Even if your left-hand opponent's 6 ♠ bid is just a wild stab, it may well require the normal heart lead to defeat it; a double would ask partner to select something else.

5. *Double.* It may be essential to set up a diamond trick before your ace of hearts is knocked out, and your solidity in diamonds makes it unlikely that the double will backfire by giving away important information to declarer.

6. *Pass.* You have no reason to believe that a diamond lead will be best for your side.

7. *Double.* If you had wanted a heart lead, you would have doubled the 3 ♡ cue-bid, so the normal lead on this auction is a club. As it happens, the opponents have misbid and are off the first two spade tricks, but they will be able to discard their spade losers on a side suit unless you cash your winners immediately.

8. *Double.* Ask partner to try and hit your solid suit by selecting his shortest holding.

9. *Pass.* A heart lead might work out well, but there is no guarantee that it will defeat the contract.

10. *Double.* Partner must have a strong spade suit to make a two-level overcall of a 1 NT opening bid, so insist that he lead his own suit. It is not unusual for the opponents to reach 3 NT with no spade stopper at all on an auction like this one, for right-hand opponent has a difficult problem with a strong balanced hand and weak spades.

Part III.

INFORMATORY DOUBLES

7

Doubles of Unusual Opening Bids

♠ ♡ ◇ ♣

All bridge players know that one important usage of the double is to increase a prospective penalty. Most also realize that there are times when the double is used to ask partner to take out to his best suit. Few, however, are aware of a third, modern usage of the double—*to give information to partner* in certain sequences where no bid will adequately describe a hand that is too strong for a pass. One example of this neoteric technique is the responsive double, which was described in Chapter 1:

YOU	LHO	PARTNER	RHO
—	1 ♡	Double	2 ♡
?			

You hold:

♠ K J 3
♡ 6 5 4 2
◇ A 10 7
♣ K 3 2

You have no good suit to bid and your hearts are far too weak for a penalty double, but your side may miss a cold partial or game if you pass. To resolve this vexing situation, many experts use a double of 2 ♡ as *informatory,* showing partner a good hand for either offense or defense and leaving the final decision to him.

The judicious use of informatory doubles is one of the hallmarks of today's knowledgeable bridge player. There is nothing complicated about such bids; the only prerequisite is to discuss matters with your partner prior to beginning play in order to be certain that both of you are using the same methods. This chapter will deal with some relatively basic procedures; the next chapter will describe some optional expert techniques for the benefit of those who wish to add the finishing touches to their competitive bidding procedures.

Doubles of Preemptive Opening Bids

STRENGTH REQUIREMENTS

The higher the level of bidding at which your right-hand opponent opens, the more strength you need to compete. However, the exact point requirements are a matter of taste and partnership agreement. Aggressive players may wish to compete with somewhat fewer points than the number suggested below, while conservative players may prefer to have a point or two extra before acting.

Preempt	Strength Needed to Act in Second Position	Strength Needed to Balance in Fourth Position
4 ♠, 5 ♣, or 5 ♦	About 18 points	About 14 points
3 ♠, 4 ♣, 4 ♦, or 4 ♡	About 17 points	About 13 points
Weak 2 ♠ bid, 3 ♣, 3 ♦, or 3 ♡	About 16 points	About 12 points
Weak 2 ♦ or 2 ♡ bid	About 15 points	About 11 points

Note that extra strength is desirable to double a spade bid because partner will have to respond at a higher level. Also, after a preempt by your *left*-hand opponent has been passed around to you, you should balance with about four points (or one trick) less than you need to act in the immediate position.

FOUR-SPADE PREEMPTS OR HIGHER

If your right-hand opponent opens the bidding with 4 ♠, you will need to have your wits about you—and a special bidding method or two up your sleeve—in order to survive the severe loss of bidding space that you have suffered. One good way to strike back is to *overcall with 4 NT to ask partner to take out to his best suit.* You are very unlikely ever to want to use the 4 NT overcall as Blackwood or take a flier on making ten tricks in notrump, so reserve it for hands like

```
♠  —
♡  K 10 6 2
♢  A Q 8 6 5
♣  A K J 8
```

This enables you to use the double of 4 ♠ as informatory, telling partner that you have a strong hand but no clear idea as to whether your side should declare or defend. A typical example would be:

```
♠  A 3 2
♡  A 8 5
♢  A K 10 4
♣  K 6 5
```

Partner will now know that he should pass and play for the probable penalty with a relatively balanced hand like either of the following:

```
♠  6 4                    ♠  6 4
♡  Q 9 6 3                ♡  9 7 6 3 2
♢  7 6 2                  ♢  7 6
♣  A 9 4 3                ♣  8 4 3 2
```

With a long suit and an offensively oriented hand, however, he will take appropriate action. For example:

(a)		(b)	
♠	7 4	♠	7
♡	K Q J 6 4 3	♡	K Q J 9 6 3
◇	3 2	◇	5 3 2
♣	Q J 10	♣	A Q 8

With hand (a), he will bid 5 ♡ in response to your informatory double of the enemy 4 ♠ bid; with hand (b), he will jump
directly to 6 ♡.

Competing against enemy preempts is a difficult task, and
there is no way to ensure success in any and all situations. The
methods just described should prove most effective in the long
run, but they do have the disadvantage of requiring you to *pass*
an opening 4 ♠ bid by your right-hand opponent with a hand
like

♠ A Q J 5
♡ A 7 2
◇ Q 6 4
♣ 7 5 3

You are virtually certain to defeat 4 ♠, but an informatory double might elicit a fatal five-level bid from your partner.
If you knew in advance that you were going to pick up this
hand, you would elect to use penalty doubles. In the absence of
a good crystal ball, however, you must take the most likely
route to profit; and hands where informatory doubles (and partner's cooperation), are desparately needed are far more frequent
than hands where you happen to hold three or four trump
tricks. Besides, there is always the chance that partner will balance with a double when 4 ♠ gets around to him, enabling you
to pass for penalties.

A double of a 5 ♣ or 5 ◊ opening bid by your right-hand opponent is also informatory. For example, double with

♠ A 6 3
♡ A Q 8 7
◊ K Q 9 2
♣ A 3

Partner is expected to take note of the high level of bidding and play for the probable penalty unless he has a good reason for bidding.

If instead you hold

♠ A 8 3
♡ A K 10 9 7 5
◊ A Q
♣ 4 3

overcall with 5 ♡. The enemy preempt has left you room for only one try, and all you need to produce a playable trump suit is something like ♡ Q 2 from your partner. Neither of the above actions is insurable with Lloyds of London, but you must act with hands as strong as these if you are ever to succeed in overcoming a preemptive opening bid. Finally, pass a 5 ♣ opening bid and settle for a small plus with a hand like

♠ A 3
♡ 7 2
◊ 8 7 6 4 2
♣ A Q 7 4

Don't risk even a mild suggestion to partner that he get into the act at the five-level.

FOUR-HEART PREEMPTS

If your right-hand opponent opens with 4 ♡, you cannot afford to use a 4 NT overcall as a three-suited takeout because you will bypass the potentially excellent contract of 4 ♠. Therefore, the double of 4 ♡ suggests a spade contract and *guarantees* at least very good three-card support. Otherwise, the double is primarily informatory, so partner should pass with a balanced hand that is unimpressive for offensive purposes. For example, you should double 4 ♡ holding

> ♠ A Q 8 6
> ♡ 7 2
> ◇ K Q J 6 2
> ♣ A 5

If instead you hold

> ♠ 3 2
> ♡ 3
> ◇ A K J 6 5
> ♣ A K 10 8 2

overcall with 4 NT. Partner will reason that you must have little interest in a spade contract because you have willfully bypassed 4 ♠, so he will select his better minor suit.

Finally, pass a 4 ♡ preempt with a hand like

> ♠ 6 3
> ♡ K Q 10 8
> ◇ K 6 3
> ♣ A Q 6 2

A double is too likely to produce a 4 ♠ response, quite possibly on a four-card suit; and while using the double for penalties would work well with infrequent hands like this one, it is losing strategy in the long run.

If partner is the one who has doubled 4 ♡, you should pass with a relatively balanced hand; a satisfactory penalty is very likely, and declaring the contract will be disastrous if your side has no good suit fit. Since partner has promised good spade support, however, you should bid 4 ♠ with

    ♠ K J 10 3
    ♡ 6 5 4
    ◇ 10
    ♣ K Q 6 3 2

If instead you hold

    ♠ K 7 3
    ♡ 3
    ◇ 5 4 3
    ♣ K Q J 8 7 3

bid 5 ♣. Caution is essential, however, with a hand like

    ♠ J 7 3
    ♡ 9
    ◇ A 10 7 4 3
    ♣ K Q 10 4

While partner's double promises spade support, he may be short in one of the minors. Don't risk a disaster by picking what may turn out to be the wrong one; use the 4 NT response as a request to the doubler to select the minor suit that he prefers.

FOUR-CLUB AND FOUR-DIAMOND PREEMPTS

Doubles of 4 ♣ and 4 ◇ opening bids are informatory; some support for the unbid majors is desirable, but good support is not guaranteed. For example, double a 4 ♣ opening bid holding

♠ A Q 8 7
♡ A 3
◇ K J 10 7
♣ A 4 2

Try to take the pressure off partner by overcalling when you have a good hand with a very good suit. For example, bid 4 ♠ over 4 ♣ with

♠ K Q 10 8 6 5
♡ A 7 3
◇ A 10 8
♣ 3

If you double and your left-hand opponent does something obnoxious like jumping to 6 ♠, you will never get your bidding untangled; and if partner properly passes the double with a balanced hand and the opponents make their contract, you will never get your excuses untangled. With a weaker hand than this, your best bet is to pass; if partner can't balance, you're unlikely to miss a game.

THREE-LEVEL PREEMPTS

Doubles of three-level preempts are also informatory. As was the case after a 4 ♡ opening bid, however, doubles of 3 ♡ and 3 ♠ preempts promise support for the unbid major. For example, if your right-hand opponent opens the bidding with 3 ♡, double with any of the following hands:

(a)	(b)	(c)
♠ K J 9 7	♠ A Q 8	♠ K 10 8 6
♡ —	♡ 7 3	♡ K 7
◇ A J 9 6 5	◇ A K 8 6 2	◇ A K Q 7
♣ K 10 4 2	♣ K 10 9	♣ A J 9

However, prefer a 3 NT overcall (natural) with a hand like

```
     ♠  K 8
     ♡  K Q 10
     ◇  A Q 9 2
     ♣  A J 10 7
```

Your support for the unbid major is weak, and you have excellent stoppers in the enemy suit. Also reject the double if you have a strongly one-suit oriented hand:

```
(a)  ♠  A K Q 6 5     (b)  ♠  A 5
     ♡  7 4 3              ♡  8 6 3
     ◇  A 8 2              ◇  A K J 9 7 4
     ♣  K 10              ♣  K 2
```

After a 3 ♡ opening bid on your right, overcall 3 ♠ with hand (a) and bid 4 ◇ with hand (b). These overcalls promise a long and strong suit, and about as much strength as is indicated by a double.

If partner is the one who has doubled an opening bid of 3 ♡, pass with either of the following hands:

```
(a)  ♠  10 8 3     (b)  ♠  A 8 3
     ♡  6 4 2           ♡  8 3 2
     ◇  J 4 2           ◇  A 4 2
     ♣  Q 6 3 2         ♣  K 5 3 2
```

A four-level contract will almost surely be disastrous with hand (a), so try to eke out a penalty. With hand (b), you should take the sure penalty since no obvious offensive spot is indicated. With any of the following hands, however, you should remove the double of 3 ♡:

```
(a)                (b)                (c)
♠  K J 6 4 2       ♠  K J 6 4 2       ♠  K 2
♡  9 5 4           ♡  9 5 4           ♡  9 5 4
◇  7 4 3           ◇  7 4 3           ◇  7 3
♣  8 2             ♣  A Q             ♣  A Q 8 7 6 3
```

A modest 3 ♠ bid is quite enough with hand (a). In the other two examples, however, you are too strong to risk partner passing below game, so bid 4 ♠ with hand (b) and jump to 5 ♣ with hand (c).

At times, game in notrump may be your best bet:

<table>
<tr><td>(a)</td><td>♠</td><td>7 2</td><td>(b)</td><td>♠</td><td>7 4 3</td></tr>
<tr><td></td><td>♡</td><td>K Q 9</td><td></td><td>♡</td><td>Q J 10 9</td></tr>
<tr><td></td><td>◇</td><td>5 4 3</td><td></td><td>◇</td><td>9 5</td></tr>
<tr><td></td><td>♣</td><td>A Q 8 6 2</td><td></td><td>♣</td><td>A 4 3 2</td></tr>
</table>

If partner has doubled a 3 ♡ bid by your left-hand opponent and your side is vulnerable, bid 3 NT (natural) with hand (a). You have the enemy suit stopped well enough to try for the nine-trick game, but not well enough to expect a nonvulnerable penalty to be more lucrative. With hand (b), however, pass regardless of the vulnerability. You are not strong enough to be confident about making 3 NT, and the opponents are likely to be in serious trouble.

WEAK TWO-BIDS

A goodly number of players use opening bids of 2 ◇, 2 ♡, and 2 ♠ as preemptive bids, showing a long and strong suit and little defensive strength (thus, a hand similar to a weak jump overcall at the two-level). If you should happen to be faced with a weak two-bid, use a direct double primarily for *takeout,* showing about 15 points or more and good takeout-double distribution. The reason for eschewing the informatory double in this situation is that it is too dangerous to permit partner to pass with a weak balanced hand, for declarer needs only eight tricks to bring home his contract.

RESPONSIVE DOUBLES

After a preemptive opening bid has been doubled and raised, the responsive double will often avoid headaches.

For example:

YOU	LHO	PARTNER	RHO
—	3 ◊	Double	4 ◊
?			

You hold:

♠ A 7 3
♡ A 7 3
◊ 6 5 4
♣ Q J 7 2

You are too strong to pass, but you have no good suit to bid and your diamonds are too weak for a penalty double. The responsive double accurately conveys this message and leaves the final decision where it belongs—with your partner.

ALTERNATIVE TREATMENTS

The methods described in this chapter are by no means in universal use. Some of the alternative treatments that you may run into at the bridge table include:

Fishbein double. This procedure, developed by well-known expert Harry Fishbein for use against *three*-level preempts, consists of two facets. First, a double is strictly for penalties, and partner is commanded to pass. Second, an overcall in the cheapest suit (for example, a 3 ♡ overcall of a 3 ◊ opening bid) asks partner to take out to his best suit; it shows at least 16 points in high cards and either a two-suited hand or a three-suiter with shortness in the enemy suit. It does *not* necessarily promise any length or strength in the bid suit, so partner must not pass. Against most opponents, informatory doubles are best because they will come up much more often, and because the overcall in the cheapest suit is likely to be needed as a natural bid. If you know that your opponents are addicted to light preempts, however, you may do well by using Fishbein against them.

Takeout Double. Some experts use doubles of preempts up to and including 4 ♡ for takeout. This procedure can be effective when the right kind of hand comes up (namely, one where you have ideal takeout double distribution and very much want partner to bid), but it is likely to cause insuperable problems whenever you hold a strong and relatively balanced hand and wish to compete without insisting that partner remove the double to his best side suit.

Cheaper minor for takeout. Some experts use the double of a preemptive opening bid for penalties and bid the cheaper *minor* suit (3 ◊ over a 3 ♣ preempt, 4 ♣ over any other three-level preempt, and 4 ◊ over a 4 ♣ preempt) to insist that partner take out to his best suit. As was the case with the Fishbein double, such methods may be useful against opponents who frequently make shaky preempts. There is also the additional advantage that major-suit overcalls retain the useful natural meaning. Against most opponents, however, informatory doubles will be the winning strategy in the long run.

3 NT for takeout. In England, it is common to use a 3 NT overcall of a three-level preempt to ask partner to bid his best suit. This enables a direct double to be used for penalties, but has the disadvantage of changing the meaning of a bid that is likely to be needed for natural purposes.

Doubles of Artificial One-Club Bids

An increasing number of bridge players are using systems in which an opening bid of 1 ♣ is strong, artificial, and forcing. This procedure has the advantage of keeping the bidding low with strong hands; but if the opponents should happen to preempt, the auction may zoom to an extremely high level before either partner can announce the identity of a long and strong suit. Therefore, it is desirable to compete against a forcing club bid whenever you can safely do so. Bidding with a scattering of high cards is dangerous, for your left-hand opponent doesn't need much strength to make a killing penalty double in view of his partner's powerful bid, but entering the auction with hands that are rich in playing strength is likely to be very effective.

One good method, devised by Alan Truscott, is to use simple overcalls to show two-suited hands and jump overcalls to show one-suited hands. His suggestion works as follows:

Over Artificial 1 ♣ Bid	Over Artificial 1 ◇ Response to Forcing 1 ♣ Bid
1 ◇ = diamonds and hearts	2 ◇ = diamonds and hearts
1 ♡ = hearts and spades	1 ♡ = hearts and spades
1 ♠ = spades and clubs	1 ♠ = spades and clubs
2 ♣ = clubs and diamonds	2 ♣ = clubs and diamonds
1 NT = diamonds and spades	1 NT = clubs and hearts
Double = clubs and hearts	Double = diamonds and spades
2 ◇, 2 ♡, 2 ♠, 3 ♣ = natural, shows suit bid	3 ◇, 2 ♡, 2 ♠, 3 ♣ = natural, shows suit bid

An easy way to remember this apparently complicated table is that a simple overcall shows the suit bid plus the *next higher* suit, a double shows the suit doubled plus the suit *two* steps higher, and a 1 NT overcall shows the two suits that could not be expressed by any of the other bids. All jump overcalls show one-suited hands. This method gives your side a good chance to find your best suit fit and preempt the bidding as quickly as possible, which is the best way to strike back against a forcing club system. For example:

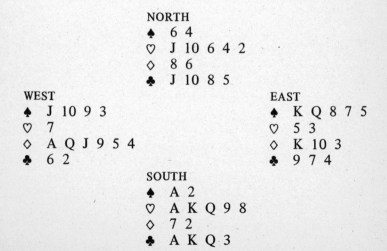

```
                    NORTH
                    ♠  6 4
                    ♡  J 10 6 4 2
                    ◇  8 6
                    ♣  J 10 8 5
    WEST                                EAST
    ♠  J 10 9 3                         ♠  K Q 8 7 5
    ♡  7                                ♡  5 3
    ◇  A Q J 9 5 4                      ◇  K 10 3
    ♣  6 2                              ♣  9 7 4
                    SOUTH
                    ♠  A 2
                    ♡  A K Q 9 8
                    ◇  7 2
                    ♣  A K Q 3
```

South, who is using a forcing club system, opens the bidding with 1 ♣ to show a powerful hand. This bid, however, provides no information whatsoever as to the location of South's long suits; he could even be void in clubs. Therefore, West properly disrupts the bidding before South can define his hand further: He overcalls with a Truscott 1 NT, showing spades and diamonds. North passes, and East makes the key bid by jumping to 4 ♠. East-West have thus found an optimal sacrifice; and poor South, who hasn't even had a chance to show his suits, may well blunder headlong into an ignominious defeat by bidding—and going down in—5 ♡.

Doubles of Strong Two-Bids

The Truscott procedure is also useful against an artificial and forcing 2 ♣ opening bid for much the same reasons. If instead the opponents are using natural strong two-bids, one possibility is to double with a distributional hand and shortness in the enemy suit in order to suggest a possible sacrifice. An alternative idea, and perhaps a superior one, is to wait until the next deal before entering the auction.

Review Quiz

Part I.

In each of the following problems, your side is vulnerable, and your right-hand opponent's opening bid is shown. What call do you make?

(1)
RHO opens 4 ♠
♠ —
♡ A K Q 7 4 2
◇ A 9 7 3
♣ A J 2

(2)
RHO opens 4 ♠
♠ K 8 7
♡ A 8 6
◇ A Q 9
♣ A J 10 9

(3)
RHO opens 4 ♠
♠ K Q 10 3
♡ 7 4
◇ A 6 2
♣ K 4 3 2

(4)
RHO opens 4 ♡
♠ A J 7 3
♡ 2
◇ K Q J 6
♣ A Q 8 5

(5)
RHO opens 4 ♡
♠ 7 4
♡ 8 6 2
◇ A J 10 6
♣ A K J 2

(6)
RHO opens 4 ♡
♠ A Q J 8 6 3
♡ 7
◇ A Q 8 4
♣ K 2

(7)
RHO opens 3 ◇
♠ K Q 9 7
♡ A 7 3
◇ K 2
♣ A 10 4 3

(8)
RHO opens 3 ◇
♠ K J 10 9
♡ K Q 10 9 5 4
◇ A 8
♣ 3

(9)
RHO opens 3 ♣
♠ 7
♡ K J 3 2
◇ K J 6 4 3
♣ A 7 4

(10)
RHO opens 2 ♠
(weak)
♠ 7 2
♡ K J 3
◇ A Q 8 4
♣ K 10 5 2

(11)
RHO opens 2 ♡
(weak)
♠ A Q 8 6
♡ 7
◇ 3 2
♣ K Q J 6 4 2

(12)
RHO opens 2 ♡
(weak)
♠ A Q J 3
♡ 7
◇ 4 2
♣ A K J 10 6 3

Part II.

In each of the following problems, your side is vulnerable, and the bidding proceeds as shown. What call do you make?

(13)	YOU — ?	LHO 4 ♡	PARTNER Double	RHO Pass	You hold: ♠ A 6 3 ♡ 7 4 2 ◇ K 5 4 2 ♣ 9 5 3

(14)	YOU — ?	LHO 3 ♡	PARTNER Double	RHO Pass	You hold: ♠ A Q 8 6 5 ♡ 7 4 3 ◇ K 6 ♣ 10 9 8

(15)	YOU — ?	LHO 4 ♠	PARTNER 4 NT	RHO Pass	You hold: ♠ 7 4 3 ♡ K Q 8 7 ◇ 9 7 6 4 ♣ 7 2

(16)	YOU — ?	LHO 4 ♡	PARTNER 4 NT	RHO Pass	You hold: ♠ K Q 8 7 ◇ 7 4 3 ◇ 9 7 6 4 ♣ 7 2

(17)	YOU — ?	LHO 4 ♡	PARTNER Double	RHO Pass	You hold: ♠ 7 4 2 ♡ 7 ◇ K J 9 7 5 ♣ A J 9 8

(18)

YOU	LHO	PARTNER	RHO	You hold:
—	2 ♠*	Double	Pass	♠ 6 3
?				♡ 5 4 3 2
	* Weak two-bid			◇ 7 6 3 2
				♣ 7 4 3

(19)

YOU	LHO	PARTNER	RHO	You hold:
—	2 ♠*	Double	Pass	♠ 7 2
?				♡ Q 10 8 6
	* Weak two-bid			◇ A 9 7 2
				♣ 6 4 3

(20)

YOU	LHO	PARTNER	RHO	You hold:
—	3 ♡	Pass	Pass	♠ A J 3
?				♡ 8
				◇ K 10 9 7 3
				♣ K 8 7 6

Solutions

1. *Four notrump.* Your heart suit is strong enough for an overcall, but why put all your eggs in one basket? Partner may have a singleton or void in hearts and a strong five-card or longer minor suit. If he bids 5 ♣ or 5 ◇, you will describe your hand and issue a strong slam invitation by bidding 5 ♡; if he jumps to 6 ♣ or 6 ◇, showing a long and strong suit, you should raise to seven.

2. *Double.* A typical informatory double, showing a good hand and leaving the decision to partner. He will pass with a relatively balanced hand and you will chalk up a penalty. If he has a strong suit and an offensively oriented hand, he will bid what should be a fine game or slam.

3. *Pass.* Had you known in advance that this was going to happen, you would have used penalty doubles; but

informatory doubles will be best in the large majority of situations.

4. *Double*. Your excellent spade support and strong hand make the double ideal.

5. *Pass*. Both your hand and your spades are too weak for a bid.

6. *Four spades*. A double would place far too much pressure on partner. He can hardly bid spades with three to the king or ten, and he might make a catastrophic pass with a relatively balanced hand.

7. *Double*. Show your strength and let partner take it from there.

8. *Three hearts*. An informatory double is out because you don't want partner to pass with a weak balanced hand, so you must overcall even though there is some risk of missing a good spade fit.

9. *Pass*. You're not strong enough for a double, and the diamond suit is too weak for an overcall. The singleton in an unbid major is also a good reason for staying on the sidelines.

10. *Pass*. This hand would be a doubtful double of *one* spade.

11. *Three clubs*. If you double for takeout, you will have to convert a 3 ♦ response to 4 ♣, and you're not strong enough to reach the four-level on a possible misfit.

12. *Double*. This time you can afford to look for a spade fit, for you are powerful enough to bid 4 ♣ over a 3 ♦ response.

13. *Pass*. Don't disturb a double of a high-level preempt with a balanced hand like this one. A satisfactory penalty is very likely, and your side may have no good suit fit at all.

14. *Four spades*. Your hand is offensively oriented, and you are just about strong enough to insist on game opposite partner's three-level informatory double.

15. *Five hearts*. Partner has asked you to bid your best suit, and you must comply with his request.

16. *Five diamonds*. Partner would have doubled had he

been interested in hearing about the spades, so select your better minor suit.

17. *Four notrump.* Partner's double guarantees spade support, but he may be able to stand only one of the minor suits. Therefore, use the 4 NT bid to ask him to pick the one he prefers. If you respond 5 ♣, he may pass with only three-card support because he expects you to have a stronger suit. A 5 ◊ bid is also inferior, for partner will have to move up to the six-level if he finds it necessary to convert to clubs.

18. *Three diamonds.* A double of a weak two-bid is for takeout, so you must bid unless you have strong trumps. The reason for not responding in the unbid major is that you don't want to do anything that has the slightest chance of getting partner excited when your hand is this weak.

19. *Three hearts.* Since you have some values, follow the standard operating procedure of bidding a major suit when you can. You won't mind if partner raises to game with extra strength.

20. *Double.* Balancing requires about one trick less than a bid in the immediate position, so you are strong enough to contest the issue. You have good support for the unbid suits, and your defense will be adequate if partner should choose to pass for penalties.

8

Expert Tactics

♠ ♡ ◇ ♣

In this chapter, we will enter the twilight zone of modern expert bidding. In particular, the use of informatory doubles will be extended to a variety of competitive bidding situations. Be forewarned, however, that the methods described here are not intended for the casual player or partnership. If you take your bridge seriously, however, you are likely to find techniques that will help you compete successfully in situations that confound and confuse all but the most expert.

Informatory Doubles: Some Advanced Situations

MAXIMAL OVERCALL DOUBLES

Suppose that the auction proceeds (neither side vulnerable):

YOU	LHO	PARTNER	RHO
1 ♠	2 ♡	2 ♠	3 ♡
?			

(a) ♠ A K J 8 6 2   (b) ♠ A K J 9 3
    ♡ 7 3   ♡ 7 4
    ◇ A 8 4   ◇ A 5 3
    ♣ 7 6   ♣ K Q 6

Hand (a) is worth much more on offense than on defense, so playing in 3 ♠ is likely to be your best course of action. You may bring home nine tricks in spite of your minimum in high cards because you are rich in playing strength, or you may register a good sacrifice by going down only one trick when the opponents are cold for 3 ♡. The problem is that if you bid 3 ♠, partner may think that you are trying for game with a hand like (b) and go on to 4 ♠ if he has a maximum for his previous bid, getting your side too high.

Matters would be much simpler if the opponents had competed in diamonds or clubs, for you could then use a 3 ♠ bid as a signoff and bid a new suit (for example, 3 ♡) to invite game. In the present situation, however, there is no room to bid a new suit because the opponents have made a "maximal" overcall—an overcall in the suit just below your own. The best way to retaliate is to use the *maximal overcall double* in order to invite game. Here's how this type of informatory double works:

1. With a hand like (b), double 3 ♡. This tells partner to bid 3 ♠ with a minimum but to jump to 4 ♠ with a maximum. Your double does not promise any heart strength, so partner may pass only if he is loaded in hearts and expects to obtain the best result by defending.

2. If you don't want partner to take any further action because you have a hand like (a), bid 3 ♠. This is a signoff, ordering him to pass even if he has a maximum for his previous bid.

Maximal overcall doubles are very useful and give up virtually nothing, for you are unlikely to gain by using this double for penalties. Even if you do happen to have a hand that is ideal for defensive purposes, such as

> ♠ A 9 4 3 2
> ♡ Q J 10 9
> ◊ A K 3
> ♣ 2

partner will probably pull a penalty double because he is void in hearts.

INFORMATORY DOUBLES IN COMPETITION

There are numerous situations in which informatory doubles are preferable to penalty doubles. Some of these include:

1. The enemy suit has been bid and raised at a low level. If the opponents have agreed on a trump suit and the auction is at only the two-level or three-level, a penalty double is unlikely to be a useful tool. Most of the cards in their suit are accounted for, so you are unlikely to hold powerful trumps; and even if you do have a trump stack, partner will probably be void and will spoil your fun by pulling the double. Therefore, your best strategy is to use such doubles as informatory. One example of this is the maximal overcall double, discussed above. Here's another:

YOU	LHO	PARTNER	RHO
–	–	1 ♡	2 ♣
2 ♡	3 ♣	Pass	Pass
?			

You hold:

♠ A 7 4 3
♡ J 6 2
◇ A 10 9 4
♣ 8 3

You have too much strength to give up the fight, but you don't know whether your side should declare or defend; your aces are useful for either offense or defense, and both your heart support and your holding in the enemy suit are weak. Partner may have a strong preference, so you should make an informatory double and let him decide what to do. The problem here is not that you need a special way to show extra strength—a bid of either 3 ♡ or 3 ◊ would do that— but that you want to reserve the option of playing for penalties if partner is so inclined. Another example:

YOU	LHO	PARTNER	RHO
—	1 ♡	1 ♠	2 ♡
?			

You hold:

♠ Q 6
♡ J 6
◊ K J 9 8 7
♣ A 10 8 7

A pass is not unthinkable, but your side may well have the balance of power. Your spade support is too meager for a raise and your minor suits are too weak to introduce at the three-level, so the best way to compete is by making an informatory double. (If instead you have a void or singleton in partner's suit, however, a discreet pass is preferable, for the deal may well be a dangerous misfit.)

2. Your previous bidding shows that you cannot be very strong in the suit that you are doubling. If your previous bidding indicates that you cannot have a booming trump holding, your double must be informatory. For example:

YOU	LHO	PARTNER	RHO
—	—	1 ◊	Pass
1 NT	2 ♠	Pass	Pass
?			

You hold:

♠ A 6 3
♥ J 7 4
♦ A 6
♣ 10 9 7 4 3

Since you failed to bid 1 ♠ at your first turn, you cannot have very strong spades. Therefore, a double is informatory, and you should make it because you have a maximum for your previous bid and a hand that is valuable for either offense or defense. Another example:

YOU	LHO	PARTNER	RHO
—	1 ♣	Pass	Pass
Double	Pass	1 ♥	2 ♣
?			

You hold:

♠ A 10 7 2
♥ A 8 6
♦ Q 9 7 4
♣ A K

You have much more strength than was promised by your balancing double, but you have no good suit to bid and your heart support is inferior. Fortunately, a double in this sequence is informatory. Why? Your original double was for takeout and showed shortness in clubs, so you cannot have a trump stack. The informatory double is preferable to a 3 ♣ cue-bid for two reasons: The cue-bid may get your side too high, and it rules out any chance of chalking up a juicy penalty by defending against 2 ♣ doubled.

3. You are doubling a low-level contract in front of declarer. If any trump honors that you hold are likely to be subject to some devastating finesses, you will rarely want to make a unilateral penalty double of a low-level contract. In this situation, therefore, a double is best treated as informatory. For example:

YOU	LHO	PARTNER	RHO
—	—	1 ♡	Pass
1 ♠	2 ◇	Pass	Pass
?			

You hold:

    ♠ K Q J 9
    ♡ 7 3
    ◇ 6 4 2
    ♣ A J 10 4

Even though partner's pass suggests a minimum opening bid, you are too strong to sell out to 2 ◇. However, it is inadvisable to rebid a four-card suit, introduce your four-card club suit at the three-level, or support hearts with such a meager holding. Thus, an informatory double is the only sensible action. If instead you hold

    ♠ A K Q 4 2
    ♡ 10 8
    ◇ 9 5 3
    ♣ K Q 6

the informatory double is also your best choice. If partner is short in spades, he will pass and play for a lucrative penalty; if he has a modicum of spade support and removes the double to 2 ♠, you can proceed directly to 4 ♠.

INFORMATORY DOUBLES OF STAYMAN RESPONSES

Consider the following situation:

YOU	LHO	PARTNER	RHO
—	1 NT	Pass	2 ♣*
?			* Stayman

Some players use a double of 2 ♣ as lead-directing, asking partner to start off with a club against the eventual enemy contract. The trouble with this treatment is that it is all too likely to backfire; the opponents have a substantial amount of strength, so they may be able to wrap up 2 ♣ (quite possibly redoubled) even with a very poor trump suit. A better plan is to use doubles of Stayman responses as informatory, showing a hand worth an opening bid but lacking a good suit in which to overcall. The advantage of this procedure is that your right-hand opponent may be bidding 2 ♣ with a Yarborough, hoping to reduce the chances of incurring a serious penalty by escaping from 1 NT before it is doubled by you. If you are using lead-directing doubles of 2 ♣, he is likely to get away with his nefarious scheme; but if you have adopted informatory doubles, you can tell partner that he should double an enemy suit contract with strong trumps even if he has very little on the side. This key item of information is likely to be just what your side needs to land a sizeable penalty.

SACRIFICE-SUGGESTING DOUBLES

On occasion, a double of an enemy cue-bid can be used to inform partner that a sacrifice against the opponents' eventual game or slam may be worthwhile. For example (only the opponents are vulnerable):

YOU	LHO	PARTNER	RHO
—	—	—	1 ♠
Pass	3 ♠	Pass	4 ◇
?			

A double in this situation cannot be lead-directional because you will be on lead against the probable spade contract. Therefore, the double shows a hand with long diamonds and little defensive strength, such as

♠   3
♡   Q J 10 9
◇   K 9 7 6 4 3
♣   7 2

It suggests to partner that the best way to cut your losses on this deal may be to sacrifice in diamonds.

Redoubles

STRENGTH-SHOWING REDOUBLES

Suppose that partner opens with 1 ♠, your right-hand opponent makes a takeout double, and you hold:

♠   6
♡   A K 8 7
◇   Q J 10 3
♣   J 10 8 2

You should redouble, showing at least 10 high-card points and suggesting that your partnership will do best by playing to penalize the opponents; and when one of them runs out to 2 ♣, 2 ◊, or 2 ♡, you should double for penalties. An initial redouble is also correct with

♠ 6 3
♡ A K 8 7
◊ K Q 10 3
♣ 4 3 2

You will be happy to double for penalties if your opponents blunder into 2 ◊ or 2 ♡. But, if your right-hand opponent escapes to 2 ♣, you should pass (which is forcing in view of your original redouble) and see if partner wants to double.

With good support for partner's suit, it is often better to avoid confusion by selecting an alternative call. For example, suppose that partner's 1 ♠ opening bid is followed by a double and you hold:

♠ Q J 9 5
♡ 7
◊ A Q 10 3
♣ 5 4 3 2

A redouble would not misrepresent your strength, but you don't particularly want to urge partner to try and penalize the opponents when your spade support is this strong. Therefore, the common expert practice is to respond 2 NT, a conventional and forcing bid that shows fine spade support and 10-12 points. A response of 3 NT is also conventional, showing excellent support for partner's suit and 13-15 points; a direct raise to 3 ♠ is preemptive and shows a hand like

♠ Q 9 8 5 4
♡ 7 6
◊ 8 4
♣ Q 10 9 3

If you happen to pick up a hand that calls for a normal jump response in notrump, you can simply redouble.

Redoubles of negative doubles also promise good overall strength. For example:

YOU	LHO	PARTNER	RHO
–	1 ♠	2 ♣	Double*
?			* Negative

Redouble with

```
♠  7 5
♡  A 10 4 2
♢  Q 10 9 6
♣  K 6 3
```

A club raise is preemptive, showing fine support but not much strength on the side. Thus, raise to 3 ♣ if neither side is vulnerable and you hold

```
♠  7
♡  6 4 3 2
♢  Q 10 9 6
♣  Q 10 6 4
```

"SOS" REDOUBLES

Technically, a redouble means that you are very confident that you will make your doubled contract and want to increase the reward. There are times, however, when you should attach the opposite meaning to a redouble and use it to inform partner that he had better bid something else because your side is in terrible trouble. For example:

YOU	LHO	PARTNER	RHO
—	—	1 ♣	Pass
Pass	Double	Pass	Pass
?			

Since you were too weak to respond to partner's 1 ♣ bid, you can't possibly have a real redouble. Even if you have a lot of clubs and keenly deduce that the opponents have made a ghastly error, your best bet is to pass quickly and grab a profit before somebody changes his mind. Therefore, a redouble in this sequence acts as an "SOS," showing extreme shortness in clubs and demanding that partner try something else. For example, redouble with:

```
♠  J 6 4 2
♡  J 9 5 4
♢  10 8 6 4 3
♣  —
```

SOS redoubles may also be useful when partner opens with 1 NT and you have a mess like

```
♠  J 6 4 3
♡  7 6 4 2
♢  9 6 4 3
♣  2
```

Perhaps nothing horrible will happen if you pass, but it is usually easier to double 1 NT for penalties than two of a suit. Your best choice is a Stayman 2 ♣ response, because you can safely pass any response by partner. If your left-hand opponent gets into the act by doubling 2 ♣ and this is passed back to you, use a redouble as an SOS, asking partner to pick one of the three unbid suits.

Some players also use SOS redoubles after partner's overcall has been doubled for penalties. This may be useful if you have a void in his suit and length in all of the others; but

with a card or two in support, it is usually best to pass and trust
that partner will turn up with a strong enough suit to avoid a
catastrophe.

PENALTY PASSES OVER REDOUBLES

Psychic redoubles are rare, but can produce devastating
results. For example:

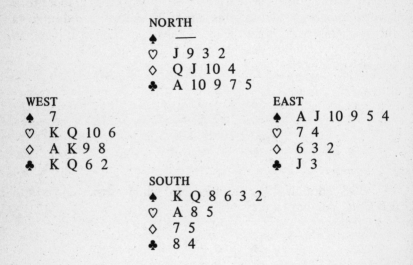

```
                        NORTH
                        ♠  —
                        ♡  J 9 3 2
                        ◊  Q J 10 4
                        ♣  A 10 9 7 5
WEST                                      EAST
♠  7                                      ♠  A J 10 9 5 4
♡  K Q 10 6                               ♡  7 4
◊  A K 9 8                                ◊  6 3 2
♣  K Q 6 2                                ♣  J 3
                        SOUTH
                        ♠  K Q 8 6 3 2
                        ♡  A 8 5
                        ◊  7 5
                        ♣  8 4
```

When South opened with a weak 2 ♠ bid and West
doubled, North knew that he was in serious trouble; the missing
spades were obviously located with East, who would happily
pass for penalties. Behaving with commendable coolness under
fire, North redoubled, acting for all the world like a man with
strong four-card spade support. East, of course, knew that
something fishy was going on and wanted to *re*redouble, but all
he could legally do was pass. South also passed, and West was
taken in; thinking that the opponents had a good spade fit, he
hurriedly pulled the double and enabled North-South to escape
a devastating penalty.

To avoid a trap like this one, some experts play that a pass
of a redouble is for penalties. Using this method, East would

pass the redouble of 2 ♠ as a command for partner to play it right there; with any hand where he did *not* want to play in 2 ♠ redoubled, he would scrape up some bid even if he had a Yarborough. To be sure, few opponents are likely to be imaginative enough to think of a redouble with the North hand, but you never can tell when you will run into such a clever adversary. In fact, unlikely as it may seem, this is a true story.

I should know; I was East.

Doubling Ethics

It is an unfortunate fact that some players resolve difficult decisions by deliberately or inadvertently adopting tactics that don't belong in any bridge game. For example, they may double quickly and loudly when they are loaded in trumps and wish to insist that partner pass, or double hesitantly and softly when they are weak in trumps and won't mind if partner decides to pull the double. Alternatively, they may think for a long time and then pass in order to let partner know that they have extra strength (else what would there be to think about?) without incurring the risk of bidding too high or doubling a cold contract. Or they may pass like lightning with a terrible hand and thereby inform partner not to play them for any extra values.

Hesitating, even at length, is perfectly legal; bridge is a tough game, and you are not expected to take an equal amount of time at every turn. However, the laws of bridge also state that *information may be conveyed only through the calls and plays that are made, and NOT by means of haste or hesitation, special emphasis or wording, facial expressions, tones of voice, or extraneous comments.* Thus, you should try always to bid and play with the same speed, emphasis, and tone; and when something unusual occurs such as a long hesitation (as it inevitably must, since we are all human), *the partner of the player who has hesitated must refuse to draw information from this extracurricular action and bend over backwards to do whatever he would have done had the hesitation not occurred.*

In sum: Restrict your bridge communications to the bids,

passes, and plays that you make, and not the way you make them. This is one expert technique that requires no special skill or memorization, but which will make you a player who is welcome in any bridge game.

Some Controversial Competitive Techniques

The merits of the competitive bidding techniques to be described in this section are highly debatable. Some have been included because they are brand new, and may represent the wave of the future; others are presented because they are interesting to read about, although not overly practical; and some of the methods discussed here are used widely enough so that you should be prepared to meet up with them at the bridge table even if you don't plan to use them yourself.

OFF-SHAPE TAKEOUT DOUBLES

Some experts advocate one-level takeout doubles with hands worth an opening bid even if the distribution is far from ideal. This camp includes no less an authority than the perennial world champion Italian Blue Team, as is shown by this deal from the 1968 World Championship Olympiad (East-West vulnerable):

NORTH
- ♠ K Q 7 2
- ♡ K J 8 5 4 3 2
- ◇ 7
- ♣ 2

WEST
- ♠ 8 6 4 3
- ♡ 10
- ◇ A K 6 3
- ♣ A Q 9 8

EAST
- ♠ —
- ♡ Q 6
- ◇ J 10 9 5 4 2
- ♣ K 10 7 6 5

SOUTH
- ♠ A J 10 9 5
- ♡ A 9 7
- ◇ Q 8
- ♣ J 4 3

SOUTH (USA)	WEST (ITALY)	NORTH (USA)	EAST (ITALY)
—	—	—	Pass
1 ♠	Double	Redouble	2 ♠
Pass	3 ♣	3 ♡	3 ♠
Pass	4 ◇	4 ♠	5 ◇
Pass	Pass	5 ♠	6 ♣
Pass	Pass	6 ♠	Pass
Pass	Double	Pass	Pass
Pass			

In spite of his singleton in the unbid major, West elected to make a takeout double of 1 ♠. How he planned to cope with a high-level response in hearts is not clear, but the eventual result was to compel North and South to concede 100 points by sacrificing in 6 ♠. In the other room, the American West passed 1 ♠: his side never got into the auction, and South landed a handsome profit for Italy by stopping in 5 ♠ and making it.

OUT-OF-THE-BLUE TAKEOUT DOUBLES

In high-level play, where capable and seasoned contestants fight furiously to obtain the slightest edge, a situation like the following can arise (opponents are vulnerable):

YOU	LHO	PARTNER	RHO
—	1 ♡	Pass	2 ♡
Pass	4 ♡	Double	Pass
?			

You hold:

♠ Q 9 6 3
♡ Q 10
◇ A J 10 5 2
♣ Q 9

Ordinarily, partner's double of a strongly bid game contract like this one would be lead-directional. But there is an excellent reason for ruling out this interpretation in the present situation: *He* is on lead. Your heart holding and the bidding also indicate that he cannot have a trump stack, so he must be suggesting a sacrifice with a hand too weak for an original takeout double. Therefore, you should bid 4 ♠. Partner's hand:

♠ K 10 4 2
♡ —
◇ K 9 4 3
♣ 10 8 4 3 2

THE NEGATIVE SLAM DOUBLE

A few experts play that a double of an enemy slam contract in a competitive auction shows *no* defensive tricks, and

asks partner to sacrifice unless he can defeat the slam in his own
hand. This contraption has been used against me three times in
tournament play (and by noted experts in each case), and my
results were:

1. Making six, doubled.
2. Making six, doubled, with an overtrick.
3. The opponents "sacrificed" at the seven-level and
   went down four, doubled, when our slam would
   have gone down.

The reason for this series of horrible results for the negative slam double is that neither defender can be sure whether a
side-suit king or queen will turn out to be a defensive trick, and
the final decision becomes little more than guesswork. Consequently, it is recommended that you avoid this disaster-prone
device.

TWO-WAY DOUBLES

The noted Los Angeles bridge expert and teacher, Eddie
Kantar, has recommended that some doubles be given a
two-way meaning—*either* takeout or penalties. Partner is sup-
posed to decipher which idea you had in mind by looking at his
holding in the enemy suit. For example:

YOU	LHO	PARTNER	RHO
1 ♠	Pass	1 NT	2 ♡
?			

(a) ♠ A K 6 4 3   (b) ♠ A K 6 4 3
    ♡ 7   ♡ K Q 10 9
    ◇ A Q 7 4   ◇ 2
    ♣ K 10 3   ♣ K 10 3

Using two-way doubles, you double with *both* (a) and (b).
If partner has three or more hearts, he assumes that you are
making a takeout double with a hand like (a); if he has two

hearts or less, he acts under the assumption that you have doubled for penalties with a hand like (b). Hopefully, partner will make the right decision most of the time, and you will score enough gains to compensate for the occasional incredible catastrophe that occurs when you wind up defending against 2 ♡ doubled with each of you holding one trump. Here's another example:

YOU	LHO	PARTNER	RHO
1 ♠	Pass	1 NT	2 ♡
?			

(c) ♠ 4 3
     ♡ A Q 10 8 5
     ◇ A K 5 4
     ♣ 10 7

(d) ♠ A 8 7 6
     ♡ 4
     ◇ K 10 9 4
     ♣ Q 9 8 7

As we saw in Chapter 4, a double of 2 ♡ is normally for penalties and shows a hand like (c). Using two-way doubles, you also double 2 ♡ with hand (d) and hope that partner's length in hearts will lead him to the right decision.

If you prefer not to use this radical technique (which is by no means as disaster-prone as it looks), the alternative is to double for takeout with hand (a), and pass with hand (b) in the hope that partner will reopen with an informatory double that will enable you to pass for penalties; and to double for penalties with hand (c), and pass with hand (d) and concede what should at most be a part-score.

THE UNUSUAL NOTRUMP

Many players use a jump overcall in notrump as a request that partner take out to his better minor suit. For example, an "unusual" 2 NT overcall of a 1 ♡ opening bid would show a hand like

$$
\begin{array}{ll}
\spadesuit & 3 \\
\heartsuit & 7\ 2 \\
\diamondsuit & K\ Q\ J\ 6\ 3 \\
\clubsuit & K\ J\ 9\ 7\ 2
\end{array}
$$

The difficulty with this technique is that the same players also overcall with an unusual 2 NT when they have a defensive powerhouse like

$$
\begin{array}{ll}
\spadesuit & 3 \\
\heartsuit & 7\ 2 \\
\diamondsuit & A\ K\ 8\ 7\ 2 \\
\clubsuit & A\ K\ J\ 4\ 2
\end{array}
$$

As a result, the unfortunate partner of the unusual notrump bidder never knows when to sacrifice and when to play for a penalty, and the partnership competitive bidding (and morale) deteriorates rapidly. If you do elect to use this device, restrict it to sacrifice-oriented hands like the first one above and select a different bid—such as a simple suit overcall—if you have substantial defensive strength.

THE STRIPED-TAIL APE DOUBLE

Doubling a contract that you know will make with overtricks may seem like an incurable case of suicidal tendencies.
Not so, says expert John Lowenthal, who offers the following
deal as evidence (North-South vulnerable):

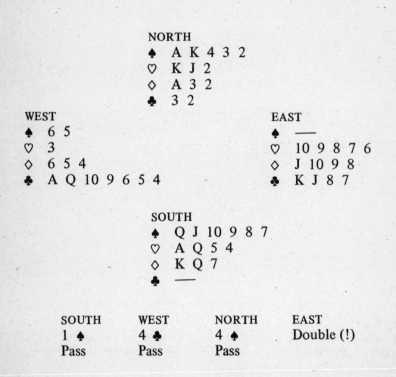

NORTH
♠ A K 4 3 2
♡ K J 2
◇ A 3 2
♣ 3 2

WEST
♠ 6 5
♡ 3
◇ 6 5 4
♣ A Q 10 9 6 5 4

EAST
♠ —
♡ 10 9 8 7 6
◇ J 10 9 8
♣ K J 8 7

SOUTH
♠ Q J 10 9 8 7
♡ A Q 5 4
◇ K Q 7
♣ —

SOUTH	WEST	NORTH	EAST
1 ♠	4 ♣	4 ♠	Double (!)
Pass	Pass	Pass	

After West's preemptive overcall, East had little doubt that
his opponents could make a grand slam, so he fiendishly doubled 4 ♠. North and South were fooled and elected to pass;
making 4 ♠ doubled with three overtricks was worth only 1390
points—considerably less than the 2210 points North and South
could have racked up by bidding the grand slam, and not even
as good as bidding and making the small slam (1460 points).
Had either North or South redoubled, East would have run back
to clubs "like a striped-tail ape" (a mythical creature that moves

very quickly), having lost nothing by his attempt to bamboozle the opponents.

Although this particular device is of value mostly for purposes of entertainment, it actually came up in an important tournament. Argentina was playing Venezuela in the 1965 South American Championships, with the winner qualifying for the 1966 World Championships (North-South vulnerable):

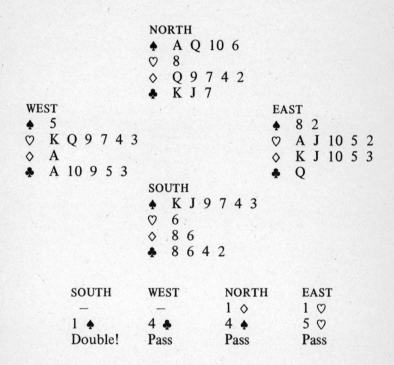

```
                    NORTH
                    ♠  A Q 10 6
                    ♡  8
                    ◇  Q 9 7 4 2
                    ♣  K J 7
WEST                                    EAST
♠  5                                    ♠  8 2
♡  K Q 9 7 4 3                          ♡  A J 10 5 2
◇  A                                    ◇  K J 10 5 3
♣  A 10 9 5 3                           ♣  Q
                    SOUTH
                    ♠  K J 9 7 4 3
                    ♡  6
                    ◇  8 6
                    ♣  8 6 4 2
```

SOUTH	WEST	NORTH	EAST
—	—	1 ◇	1 ♡
1 ♠	4 ♣	4 ♠	5 ♡
Double!	Pass	Pass	Pass

South's apish double completely fooled his opponents. They scored 850 points in 5 ♡ doubled, but the East-West pair in the other room bid 6 ♡ and racked up 1010 points. It would be nice to conclude this story by saying that the gain of 160 points was just enough to win the match for South. However, as it happens, his team (Argentina) lost by a narrow margin and Venezuela went on to the world championship. Although anticlimactic, this is not too surprising. After all, how could a striped-tail ape play in a world championship?

Epilogue

Doubles for Profit

♠ ♡ ◊ ♣

"I think I see why I've been having so many problems with doubles," my bridge-addicted friend admitted.

"Good," I said, delighted to get a word in edgewise at long last. "Let's go through those hands once again, this time highlighting the winning approach in each case."

IDEA NO. 1. THINK *TWO* STEPS AHEAD
IN COMPETITIVE AUCTIONS

"When my right-hand opponent opens the bidding with 1 ◊," my friend began, "and I hold

♠   K 4 3
♡   A K Q 6 2
◊   7
♣   Q 9 5 3

my *two*-stage battle plan should be to overcall 1 ♡ the first time and then make a subsequent takeout double if the opportunity presents itself. This will inform my partner that I have a good heart suit (and will readily enable us to locate an important 5-3 fit if one exists) plus a hand with some support for the unbid suits. For example, the auction might proceed

SOUTH	WEST	NORTH	EAST
—	—	—	1 ◇
1 ♡	2 ◇	Pass	Pass
Double			

or it might go

SOUTH	WEST	NORTH	EAST
—	—	—	1 ◇
1 ♡	Pass	Pass	2 ◇
Double			

"My partner will now support hearts, rather than bid spades, with three-card heart support and a four-card spade suit such as A 10 7 6—which is just what I want him to do. Also, he'll get his chance to mention a five-card or longer spade suit if he has one, because my second-round double assures him that it will be safe to enter the auction even with bad heart support and only a fair hand. And if he happens to be loaded in diamonds, he can convert my double to a penalty double by passing. I may not get to make my second-round double in some situations, but this price is well worth it because I avoid the agony of having to guess which suit to play in at a high level—as so often happens when I make a direct takeout double on hands like this!"

IDEA NO. 2. USE YOUR USUAL COMPETITIVE METHODS WHEN BALANCING IN FOURTH SEAT

"I also like Edgar Kaplan's idea of putting first things first when balancing in fourth seat," my friend went on. "So if my left-hand opponent opens with 1 ◇ and the next two players pass, I'll overcall 1 ♡ holding

♠ 9 3
♡ A K 7 4 2
◇ J
♣ A Q 10 9 2

just as I would in the direct position. Of course, I've clarified this with my partner prior to beginning play (and also informed the opponents, in advance, of our unusual treatment). Thus, partner knows I have some values and can act accordingly, for with a mediocre 8-12 point hand and a mediocre suit I'd have balanced with one notrump (the one important bid that does take on a new meaning in the balancing position). This lets me describe a crucial aspect of my hand before the auction gets too high. Furthermore, if instead I hold a hand like

♠ K 8 6 3
♡ Q 9 6 2
♦ 4
♣ A J 4 3

I balance with a double, promising support for all unbid suits just like the direct takeout double would do. No preempt by the opponents can embarrass us now! And I don't have to invent a whole slew of new competitive bidding methods for a situation that arises rather infrequently."

IDEA NO. 3. DON'T ALERT A GOOD DECLARER
TO A TRUMP STACK JUST TO
TRY FOR AN EXTRA 50 OR 100 POINTS

"I also agree," my friend conceded, "that I should *not* double 6 ♠ against strong opponents holding

♠ Q J 10 8
♡ K 10 3
♦ 9 8 2
♣ K 6 3

Even if I'm right, I don't stand to gain more than 50 or 100 points. A competent declarer, warned by my double, probably won't go down more than one. And the double will cost at least 1000 points—the difference between making the slam and going down — if it advises the declarer about the bad trump split in time for him to take an unusual, but winning, line of play. Which is just what happened to me!"

"Even experts go wrong on this one," I said. "I remember a match from the 1965 Spring National Knockout Teams where I brought home a 4 ♠ contract by playing for trumps to divide 5-0 after a double like the one you made. The common factor in both situations was that the trump suit had been bid *and raised*, indicating the possibility of some flexibility in playing the suit — and the inadvisability of revealing the bad trump break too early."

"Very erudite," my friend said admiringly. "And you picked up a huge gain on the board?"

"Mrmgrmpf," I mumbled, hoping for a change of topic.

"Eh? I asked how you did on the board."

"My teammates also blew their cover by doubling, and our world-famous opponent also brought home the contract," I sighed. "No swing!"

IDEA NO. 4. DON'T MAKE A PENALTY DOUBLE UNTIL YOU HAVE BID YOUR LIMIT IN YOUR SIDE'S SUIT

"I also have to admit," my friend confessed, "that it's pretty ghastly to double a 2 ♢ overcall of partner's 1 ♠ opening bid holding

♠   J 10 7 4
♡   J 9 8
♢   A K 3 2
♣   10 9

In fact, it's wrong for at least *five* reasons!

"1. We can certainly make two or more spades, and it's incorrect to make a penalty double until we've bid the limit in our own suit unless I can see a sure profit.

"2. Partner's spade strength will be mostly useless for defensive purposes in view of my length in the suit; declarer will surely start ruffing very soon.

"3. I don't have any nasty surprises for declarer. He knew he was missing the ace and king of trumps when he overcalled.

"4. The vulnerability is wrong. We're vulnerable and they are not, so it figures to be much more lucrative to go after our own game.

"5. The double of a low-level overcall promises shortness in opener's suit. Partner may misdefend as a result of my unexpected spade length and hand the opponents their contract.

"So," he continued sheepishly, "it's pretty clear that I should raise spades instead of doubling, after which we quickly get to 4 ♠."

"Quite right," I agreed. "Let's look at what would have happened had you held a hand that was really worth a double of 2 ♢:

NORTH
- ♠ J 9 6 4
- ♡ J 10 8 2
- ◇ Q 6
- ♣ 10 9 5

WEST
- ♠ 8
- ♡ K 9 6 5 4
- ◇ J 10 3
- ♣ A 7 3 2

EAST
- ♠ A K Q 5 2
- ♡ A 3
- ◇ 9 4
- ♣ Q J 8 6

SOUTH
- ♠ 10 7 3
- ♡ Q 7
- ◇ A K 8 7 5 2
- ♣ K 4

SOUTH	WEST	NORTH	EAST
—	—	—	1 ♠
2 ◇	Double	Pass	Pass
Pass			

"The double would really be ideal if you held four diamonds to the jack-ten," I went on, "but it's quite deadly just as it is. You lead a spade, and East cashes his three winners (which survive largely because of your shortness) and switches to the queen of clubs. Your side wins two club tricks and cashes the ace and king of hearts, whereupon you lead a heart for East to ruff with his nine-spot. This promotes a trump trick for you, so 2 ◇ doubled goes down three—and you rack up 500 points with no game your way."

IDEA NO. 5. INCLUDE THE FORCING PASS IN YOUR ARSENAL OF BIDDING WEAPONS

"I also goofed," my friend admitted, "when I (South) held

♠ A K 6 5 2
♡ A 7
◇ K 7 3
♣ 7 6 4

and the bidding went

SOUTH	WEST	NORTH	EAST
1 ♠	4 ♡	4 ♠	5 ♡
Double?	Pass	Pass	Pass

"We're vulnerable and the opponents aren't, so making our game figures to be more lucrative than doubling the opponents. My aces and kings are good for either offense or defense, so I should let my partner decide what to do by making a forcing pass—forcing because it can't make sense for us to accept an undoubled penalty after opting for a vulnerable game. If partner stretched to bid 4 ♠ or has a defensively oriented hand, he'll double. With his actual hand,

♠ Q J 7 3
♡ 6 4
◇ A Q J 5
♣ A 3 2

he'll be delighted to accept my invitation and bid 5 ♠ in view of his fine hand, good spade support, and weakness in the enemy suit."

"Exactly," I agreed. "Your partner was correct to pass your double, which actually showed a minimum opening bid best suited to defense, such as

♠ A K 6 5 2
♥ Q J 10
♦ 8 3
♣ K 6 5

or even

♠ K 10 6 4 2
♥ 7 3
♦ K 3
♣ K Q 10 5

"With the first hand," I went on, "5 ♠ is almost sure to go down because the diamond finesse rates to lose on the bidding; and with the second hand, you're off the first three tricks. In either case, therefore, your best strategy is to defend, and you let partner know this by doubling 5 ♥."

IDEA NO. 6. DON'T CONFUSE YOUR OWN LEAD-DIRECTING DOUBLES JUST TO TRY FOR AN EXTRA 50 OR 100 POINTS

My friend was showing signs of discomfort, but he continued bravely. "I also bungled things," he said, "when I (East) held

♠ A 4 2
♥ J 10 7 4 2
♦ —
♣ J 10 9 7 3

and the bidding proceeded

SOUTH	WEST	NORTH	EAST
1 ♠	Pass	2 ♥	Pass
3 ♠	Pass	4 ♠	Pass
4 NT	Pass	5 ♦	Double
6 ♠	Pass	Pass	Double?
Pass	Pass	Pass	

"I made the same mistake I made a few hands back—I doubled a slam just to try for an extra hundred points or so. Since the difference between making the slam and going down is over a thousand points, my only concern should be to obtain the killing lead; so *all* doubles should be lead-directional. In this situation, I can command any lead that I want! Here's how:

Lead Desired	Procedure
Heart	Double 6 ♠ only (suggests the lead of dummy's first-bid side suit)
Diamond	Double 5 ♦ only
Club	Double 5 ♦ *and* double 6 ♠ (the second double cancels the first message)

"After all," my friend continued, "I'd be dying for a *club* lead if I held

```
♠  A 4 2
♡  J 10 7 4 2
♦  J 10 9 7 3
♣  ——
```

and the 'double double' procedure is the only way I can make sure that I get it. On the actual hand, therefore, I should have passed 6 ♠."

"Don't feel too bad," I consoled him. "Experts go wrong here also. For example, suppose you hold:

```
♠  6 3
♡  Q J 9 8 2
♦  ——
♣  Q 9 8 7 5 2
```

"With only the opponents vulnerable, the bidding proceeds:

YOU	LHO	PARTNER	RHO
—	1 ♠	2 ♡	6 ♠
7 ◇!	7 ♠	Pass	Pass
?			

Your clever lead-directing bid of 7 ◇ was quite safe, of course; the opponents couldn't afford to let you play there undoubled when they're cold for a vulnerable small slam, so you'd have time to escape to your planned sacrifice of 7 ♡. Now that they've fallen into your trap, what do you do?"

"I *pass*!" my friend decided. "Partner will surely lead a diamond so long as I don't confuse the issue by doubling!"

"Right!" I agreed. "According to the May, 1968, *Bridge World,* twenty-four out of thirty-six expert panelists to whom this problem was submitted agree that if you now double 7 ♠, you demand an unusual lead (and therefore *not* a diamond). Looks like you've got the idea!"

IDEA NO. 7. REMEMBER THAT DIRECT DOUBLES OF PREEMPTIVE OPENING BIDS ARE *INFORMATORY*

"I also failed to realize," my friend continued ruefully, "that a direct double of a preemptive opening bid is *not* for takeout in the same way as a direct double of a one-level opening bid would be. If my left-hand opponent opens 1 ♠ and partner doubles, I obviously have to bid 2 ♡ holding

♠　6 4
♡　Q 9 6 3
◇　7 6 2
♣　A 9 4 3

"His double is for takeout, so it would be absurd to pass. When partner doubles a 4 ♠ opening bid, however, he may not have ideal support for all unbid suits because he's been compelled to act under extreme pressure. Also, since the opponents have bid spades, he would have overcalled with 4 NT if he wanted to insist that I bid my best suit. Therefore, I should pass unless I have a good suit of my own, or a very strong hand that suggests a slam."

"That's right," I said. "Let's look at the complete deal once more:

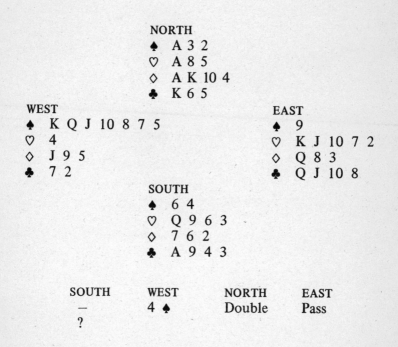

NORTH
♠ A 3 2
♡ A 8 5
◊ A K 10 4
♣ K 6 5

WEST
♠ K Q J 10 8 7 5
♡ 4
◊ J 9 5
♣ 7 2

EAST
♠ 9
♡ K J 10 7 2
◊ Q 8 3
♣ Q J 10 8

SOUTH
♠ 6 4
♡ Q 9 6 3
◊ 7 6 2
♣ A 9 4 3

SOUTH	WEST	NORTH	EAST
—	4 ♠	Double	Pass
?			

"If you correctly pass, 4 ♠ doubled goes for 500—and there's no game your way."

IDEA NO. 8. USE LOW-LEVEL DOUBLES MADE IN *FRONT* OF THE SUIT BIDDER, OR AFTER THE OPPONENTS HAVE BID *AND RAISED* THEIR SUIT, AS *INFORMATORY*

"Finally," my friend sighed, "I (West) was actually wrong to pass holding

♠ 10 8 3
♡ A K 6 4 2
◇ 7
♣ A 10 4 2

after the auction

SOUTH	WEST	NORTH	EAST
—	1 ♡	Pass	1 ♠
2 ◇	Pass	Pass	Double
Pass	?		

"Partner's double, made in front of the diamond bidder where he can be easily finessed, is informatory rather than for penalties; it simply shows a good hand and asks for my cooperation. Since my own diamonds are very weak, I should support his suit by bidding 2 ♠. If he holds

♠ A K Q 4 2
♡ 10 8
◇ 9 5 3
♣ K Q 6

he'll jump straight to 4 ♠."

"Actually, you should have bid 2 ♠ directly over 2 ◇," I pointed out. "But as it went, the deal is a good example of the modern informatory double. Here's what would have happened had you held a hand really worth a pass opposite the same hand your partner doubled with:

NORTH
♠ J 9 8 7 5
♡ Q J 7 5
◇ 7
♣ 8 5 3

WEST
♠ 10
♡ A K 6 4 2
◇ J 10 2
♣ A 10 4 2

EAST
♠ A K Q 4 2
♡ 10 8
◇ 9 5 3
♣ K Q 6

SOUTH
♠ 6 3
♡ 9 3
◇ A K Q 8 6 4
♣ J 9 7

SOUTH	WEST	NORTH	EAST
—	1 ♡	Pass	1 ♠
2 ◇	Pass	Pass	Double
Pass	Pass	Pass	

"It shouldn't be hard to collect eight defensive tricks," I said. "You've got seven top winners, and after collecting them you can .promote an extra trick if East ruffs a heart with his nine of diamonds or if East leads a fourth spade at trick eight. So here again, you rack up 500 points with no game your way."

"I begin to see why experts win more," my friend observed. "They use doubles flexibly, as the situation requires, rather than saving them for the one time in a thousand when they hold six tricks in the opponent's suit."

"Which is usually a wasted bid anyway," I added, "since someone is almost certain to pull the double. After all, if you have six trump tricks and your opponent has bid the suit, someone else is probably void—and very unhappy about the contract!"

"Right!" my friend agreed. "So let's end with . . ."

IDEA NO. 9. ADOPT MODERN PROCEDURES SUCH AS NEGATIVE, RESPONSIVE, AND MAXIMAL OVERCALL DOUBLES

"These methods will add even more expert flexibility to my bidding," my friend concluded.

"I agree," I said, "although I suspect there will always be some bridge devotees who can't tolerate the idea of using a double of an enemy overcall for takeout. But you'll be one up on them—especially since you've obviously learned a great deal about using doubles for takeout, penalties, lead direction, and cooperation."

"And," said my friend, determined to have the last word before heading off for his usual rubber bridge game, "for profit!"

Index

Aces, undervalued by point count, 19*n*
Allinger, Paul, 39
Astro Cue-Bid, 39
  responding to, 62

Balanced hand in fourth position, 89-91
Balancing, definition of, 109*n*
Balancing double
  in fourth position, 84-89, 262-63
    responding to, 91-93
  in second position, 30-31
    responding to, 50-51
Becker, B. J., 203
Becker, Michael, 203
Bernstein, Andy, 203
Blackwood responses, doubling of, 204-5
  after partner has doubled, 206
Bridge World, The, 2, 93, 94, 119, 135, 270

Cue-bids, 39-41
  doubles of, 162
    in slam contracts, 201-4
    sacrifice-suggesting, 245-46
  in fourth position, 91
  jump, 54*n*
  responding to, 60-63

Ethics of doubling, 251-52

Fishbein double, 229
Fishbein, Harry, 229
Fisher, Dr. John W., 210
Fisher double, 210
Forcing auctions, 171-73
Forcing pass, 177-81, 266-68
Frey, Dick, 10

Game contracts, strongly bid, doubles of, 207-12

Informatory doubles, 217-46
  in competition, 241-45
  maximal overcall, 239-41, 274
  of artificial one-club bids, 230-32
  of preemptive opening bids, 220-30, 270-71
    four-diamond or four-club, 225-26
    four-heart, 224-25
    four-spade or higher, 221-23
    three-level, 226-28
    for takeout, 230
    weak two-level, 228
  sacrifice-suggesting, 245-46
  of Stayman responses, 245

Insufficient bid, doubling of,
        159-60
Italian Blue Team, 252

Jacks, overvalued by point count,
        19n

Kantar, Eddie, 255
Kaplan, Edgar, 140, 262
Kings, undervalued by point count,
        19n

Lead-directing doubles, 195-212
        268-70
    in slam auctions, 196-206
    of strongly bid game contracts,
        207-12
Lightner double, 210, 211
Lowenthal, John, 258

Mason, David, 143
Mastola, Frank, 144
Maximal overcall double, 239-41
        274
Michaels, Mike, 39
Michaels Cue-Bid, 39
    responding to, 60-61
Miles, Marshall, 211

Negative double, 118-24, 274
    responding to, 124-26
Negative slam double, 254-55
Nonforcing auctions, 181-82
Notrump bid
    double after 1 NT/3 NT,
        207-8, 210

double after strongly bid 3 NT,
        208-10
    opening, double of, 162-63, 188
    penalty double after partner's,
        158-59
Notrump overcall
    doubling of, 161-62, 187
    responding to, 59-60
    3 NT, for takeout, 230
    unusual, 257

Off-shape takeout double, 252-53
One-club bids, artificial, doubles of,
        230-32
Out-of-the-blue takeout double,
        254
Overcall
    after pass, 29-30
    after takeout double, 23-27
    cue-bid as, 41
    doubling after, 37-39
        responding to, 58-59
    imperfect, 37, 83
    notrump
        doubling of, 161-62, 187
        responding to, 59-60
        3 NT, for takeout, 230
        unusual, 257
    preemptive, 32-33
        in fourth position, 83
        responding to, 51-52
    regular, 34-35
        in fourth position, 83
        responding to, 54-57
    suit, doubling of, 160-61,
        184-87
    super-strong, 35-36
        in fourth position, 83
        responding to, 57
    takeout double vs., 13-18
    vulnerability and, 42
    weak jump, 33-34
        in fourth position, 83
        responding to, 53

Pass
    doubling after, 27-29
        responding to, 49-50
    forcing, 177-81, 266-68
    overcalling after, 29-30
Penalty double, 135-63
    bidding limit before, 264-66
    boomeranging of, 137-48
    flexible, 160-63
    informatory doubles as
            preferable to, 241-45
    strategy for, 149-56
    unilateral, 156-60
        bidding after partner's,
            182-84
Point count, aces and kings
        undervalued by, 19n
Preemptive bid
    opening, double of, 220-30,
            270-71
        four-diamond or four-club,
            225-26
        four-heart, 224-25
        four-spade or higher, 221-23
        three-level, 226-28
        for takeout, 230
        weak two-level, 228
    penalty double after partner's,
            156-57
    responsive double after double
            of, 228-29
Preemptive overcalls, 32-33
    in fourth position, 83
    responding to, 51-52
Psychic redouble, 250-51

Queens, overvalued by point count,
        19n

Rebids by takeout doubler, 63-64

Redoubles, 246-51
    penalty passes over, 250-51
    "SOS," 248-50
    strength-showing, 246-48
Reopening, definition of, 109n
Reopening double, 107-15
    responding to, 115-18
Responsive double, 46-49, 274
    after preemptive opening, 228-29
Rosler, Lawrence, 39
Roth, Alvin, 41, 119
Roth Cue-Bid, 41
    responding to, 62-63
Rubens, Jeff, 203

Sacrifice-suggesting doubles, 245-46
Scoring system, doubling or
        overcalling in terms of,
            42-43
Seidman, Sol, 142
Slam contracts
    doubles of, 196-204
        negative, 254-55
    striped-tail ape double as defense
            against, 258-59
Stayman response, double after,
        210
    informatory, 245
Stern, Roger, 39
Stone, Tobias, 119
Striped-tail ape double, 258-59

Takeout double
    balancing, see Balancing double
        in fourth position, 73-83
            responding to, 83-84
    ideal, 18-20
    imperfect, 21-23
    off-shape, 252-53
    out-of-the-blue, 254
    overcalling after doubling, 23-27
    overcalling, then doubling, 37-39

Takeout double, *cont.*
    responding to, 58-59
   rebids by doubler after, 63-64
    responding to, 43-46
    after interference, 46-49
  vs. overcall, 13-18
  vulnerability and, 42
Taking charge by bidding, 173-77
Truscott, Alan, 231
Two-bid
  penalty double after partner's,
    157-58

Two-bid, *cont.*
  strong, double after, 232
  weak, double after, 228
Two-suited hand
  cue-bid for, 41
  Truscott method to show, 231
Two-way double, 255-56

Vulnerability, doubling vs.
    overcalling and, 42